PULPITING THE ALTAR

REVISED

Pursuing An Open Heaven

by
Al Houghton

Purifying the Altar Revised
© 1990, 2007, 2010 by Al and Jayne Houghton
All rights reserved.
ISBN: 978-0-940252-097

Published by:
WORD AT WORK MINISTRIES INC.
P.O. Box 366
Placentia, CA 92871
www.workatwork.org   714-996-1015

All rights reserved. This book is protected under the copyright laws of the United States of America. No part of this publication may be reproduced, stored on a retrieval system, or transmitted in any way by any means electronic, mechanical, photocopy, recording, or otherwise, without the express permission of the copyright holder.

Author's Note: Capitalization of certain words are for emphasis only.

All scripture quotations, not otherwise indicated, are from *The New King James Version*, © 1982 by Thomas Nelson, Inc. Used by permission.

Second Printing, November 1995
Third Printing, May 1999
Fourth Printing, Revised 2007
Fifth Printing, Revised 2010

Reproduction of cover or text in whole or in part without the express written consent by the authors is unlawful according to the 1976 United States Copyright Act.

Printed in the United States of America.

DEDICATION

This manuscript was pioneered in the trenches of church experience. The repercussions of voicing principles that prove oppositional to tradition have a price only eternity can weigh. When called into ministry, we commit to shout from the housetops what we hear whispered in the ear. That price does not just fall on the one whose voice makes it audible; it falls on everyone around them. This book is gratefully dedicated to Jayne, Jonathan, Julie and Michael, while not understanding the warfare this message engendered, nevertheless faithfully endured while it was pioneered. The revelation of God's Word is an essential part of the development of an end-time generation completely sold out to God's purpose and plan. The generation that finishes the age has to represent Jesus "The Judge." They must valiantly display the justice Jesus bought and paid for through His death, burial and resurrection. The truths in this book make it possible to stand in the fire they have to call down. With the hope that this emerging generation will fulfill Psalm 2:8–9, "Ask of Me, and I will give You the nations for your inheritance and the ends of the earth for your possession. You shall break them with a rod of iron; you shall dash them in pieces like a potters vessel," this book is gratefully offered to the Body of Christ.

CONTENTS

PART I
PURIFYING THE CORPORATE ALTAR

CHAPTER 1
WHAT IS AN ALTAR? 3
    Famous Altars 4
    Men's Hearts Revealed 6

CHAPTER 2
THE COVENANTAL DEVELOPMENT OF
THE TITHE 11

CHAPTER 3
THE HALF-TRUTH LIE 19
    God's Provision for Harvest 20
    Preaching a Half-Truth 22
    Two Kingdoms 27
    Identifying With an Altar 31
    An Impure Prophet 35

CHAPTER 4
COVENANT-DESTROYING TRADITION 41
    False Pastors 42
    The Levitical Ministry 46
    A New Accountability 49
    "The Tithe Is Mine" 50
    Tithing Today 53
    Twelve Corrupting Influences 55
    Spiritual Politicians 56
    The Hireling Mentality 57

CHAPTER 5
   MANIPULATION, A MAJOR ROOT OF
   IMPURITY 61
      God's Way Works 62
      The Spirit of Manipulation 65
      Classes in Fund-raising 66
      When to Walk Out 68
      Motives for Publishing 69
      True Apostles and Prophets 73
      Paul's Pure Standard 74

CHAPTER 6
   THE OFFERING 79
      God's Plan for Giving 81
      Recognize Manipulation 84
      The Tithe 86
      Commanding the Blessing 88
      Free From Financial Pressures 90

CHAPTER 7
   THE SPIRIT OF AMMON 95
      When Ministry Is Thwarted 100
      Defiling the Altar 103

CHAPTER 8
   THE ANOINTING TO SPOIL 107
      Building With Satan's Money 109
      Majoring in the Wrong Rapture 111
      Financing the Harvest 113
      Pure Altars Needed 114
      Pastoring Your Business 116

CHAPTER 9
   PREPARING TO SPOIL 121

  Pastoring Mighty Men 121
  Faithfulness Disregarded 123
  David Lu's Testimony 124
  Into Temptation and My Downfall 126
  Repentance and Restoration 127
  God Made a Way 128

CHAPTER 10
 JUDGING RIGHTEOUS JUDGMENT 133
  Judging Ourselves 135
  Selling the Anointing 136

CHAPTER 11
 SEEING GOD 141
  Blueprint for Ministry 143
  A Righteous Gentile Is Honored 144
  What Financial Pressure Reveals 145
  Giving With Strings Attached 147
  How and When to Receive 149
  The Disappearing Donor 151

PART II
PURIFYING THE PERSONAL ALTAR

CHAPTER 12
 PURIFYING THE HEART "MOTIVATION" 157
  The Spirit of Balaam at Work 162
  The Altar of the Heart 164

CHAPTER 13
 "POWER OF OFFENSES" 179
  The Power of Agreement 191

CHAPTER 14
 DEVELOPING PEACE-FILLED RELATIONSHIPS .. 201

Suggested Prayer 205

CHAPTER 15
"CULTIVATING REPROOF" 209

CHAPTER 16
THE PRICE OF GENERATING A WAVE! 219

CHAPTER 17
CULTIVATING CHARACTER THAT COUNTS 227

CHAPTER 18
"JUDGMENT" 241

CHAPTER 19
NAVIGATING A DYSFUNCTIONAL FAMILY 251

CHAPTER 20
THREE LEVELS OF JUDGMENTS 259
   "Verbal Accountability" 259
   Qualifying to Execute Covenant Justice 265
   Temple Cleansing Exposure 267

CHAPTER 21
THE POWER OF THE PURIFIED ALTAR 273

CHAPTER 22
HOW STRONG CHRISTIANS GROW WEAK. 281

PRAY AND OBEY 296

BIBLIOGRAPHY 298

PART I

PURIFYING THE CORPORATE ALTAR

CHAPTER 1

WHAT IS AN ALTAR?

When a New Testament believer hears the word "altar," the first image which usually comes to mind is one of animal sacrifice. While animal sacrifices were a definite part of what happened at some of the altars in the Old Testament, there was a much larger dimension of spiritual activity. The patriarchs built their own altars, and almost always erected one to commemorate an event in which they had met with God. Altars commemorated receiving a revelation, a promise, or making vows.

After the flood, Noah had some serious business to discuss with the Lord.

> *So Noah went out, and his sons and wife and his sons' wives with him. Every beast, every creeping thing, every bird, and whatever creeps on the earth, according to their families, went out of the ark. Then Noah built an altar to the Lord, and took of every clean animal and of every clean bird, and offered burnt offerings on the altar. And the Lord smelled a soothing aroma. Then the Lord said in His heart, "I will*

never again curse the ground for man's sake, although the imagination of man's heart is evil from his youth; nor will I again destroy every living thing as I have done. "While the earth remains, seedtime and harvest, And cold and heat, And winter and summer, And day and night Shall not cease."
—Genesis 8:18–22

We are still enjoying the blessing of the promise God gave Noah. The law of seedtime and harvest still works. Without it, we could not buy what we want from the grocery store. God gave covenant promises, direction, and blessing to one who worshipped at an altar.

The Father reveals Himself in the Old Testament as the God of Abraham, Isaac, and Jacob. The sum and substance of His dealing, maturing, and revealing always produced the same response. It was in those places the patriarchs built an altar to commemorate meeting God. Altars were built where covenants were made!

Famous Altars

Abram built several altars, but perhaps the most famous was the one on which he prepared to sacrifice his son. When asked by Isaac, "Where is the lamb?" he received a revelation of the ministry of Jesus and said, "My son, God will provide for Himself the lamb for a burnt offering" (Genesis 22: 7–8). This revelation came at an altar!

Years later, when Moses received the Law at Mt. Sinai, God gave specific plans for two altars. The brazen altar was the very first thing every worshipper saw when entering the Tabernacle, because it was placed in the outer court right in front of the Tabernacle entrance. It signified man had no access to God except as a sinner atoned for through the shedding of blood!

The second altar, the altar of incense, was in the Holy Place, right in front of the veil which marked the entrance into the Holy of Holies. To walk into God's presence, you had to pass the altar of incense and walk through the veil.

This altar taught that enjoying the real presence of God is only available to the true worshippers who praise and worship from a pure heart. Worship truly is the doorway to His presence, while the veil is our flesh. When we determine to praise and worship regardless of how we feel, the door opens to God's presence. The first Tabernacle was a physical picture of the importance of altars in doing business with God.

When Naaman the Syrian obeyed the prophet's command, healing came with a revelation of the true God. Once the true was recognized, the next order of business was obtaining a pure place where he could worship. Second Kings 5:15-17 says:

> And he returned to the man of God, he and all his aides, and came and stood before him; and he said, "Indeed, now I know that there is no God in all the earth, except in Israel; now therefore, please take a gift from your servant." But he said, "As the Lord lives, before whom I stand, I will receive nothing." And he urged him to take it, but he refused. So Naaman said, "Then, if not, please let your servant be given two mule-loads of earth; for your servant will no longer offer either burnt offering or sacrifice to other gods, but to the Lord. . . .

The two mule-loads of earth would form his altar upon which to approach his newfound God with thanksgiving. Naaman was determined to no longer deal with the counterfeit because he had found the real. I believe this story bears great prophetic truth for every generation of the Body of Christ as it transitions from one season to the next.

Men's Hearts Revealed

The Lord revealed integrity of heart. Naaman's heart was also revealed. He refused to worship any other God but the Lord. Elisha's heart was revealed. He had the opportunity to profit from the anointing accompanying his office, but refused. Gehazi's heart was revealed. He chose to fund-raise, manipulate, and profit from God's anointing.

I believe, once again, God is revealing hearts!

Those who have Gehazi's heart will find the leprosy of judgment clinging to them. Gehazi became an example, for all to see, of what happens to those who set their heart on money. The attitude characterized by Gehazi makes an altar impure!

Several years ago I was given a copy of *An American Dictionary of the English Language,* published by Noah Webster in 1828,[1] before humanistic scholarship edited out our Christian faith. A high percentage of the definitions have biblical backgrounds. The definition of "altar" is extremely interesting:

1. A mount; a table or elevated place, on which sacrifices were anciently offered to some deity.
2. In modern churches, the communion table; and, figuratively, a church.
3. In scripture, Christ is called the altar of Christians, He being the atoning sacrifice for sin.

I like Webster's second definition, "In modern churches, the communion table; and, figuratively, a church." When we talk about "purifying the altar," we are talking about accepting God's purpose, correction, and reproof and walking with Him accord-

---

[1]. *American Dictionary of the English Language,* Noah Webster 1828. *Noah Webster's First Edition of an American Dictionary of the English Language.* Published by the Foundation for American Christian Education. Copyright 1967.

ingly in our homes, businesses, and churches.

The purpose of this book, *Purifying the Altar*, deals with transformation of the heart from self-seeking to servanthood, and from tradition to deliverance. Both self-seeking and tradition are elements that hinder God's purpose, while lying under the surface seemingly undetected.

Just as God met with Abraham, Isaac, and Jacob to direct, mature, correct, and lead them toward His perfect will and plan, so He meets with us for the same purpose. The sum and substance of His dealings are the fruit of the time we spend at our personal and corporate altars.

If an individual altar is pure, but joined to a corporate (church or ministry) altar that is impure, the second will dramatically affect the first. If we attend a church affiliated with any organization or denomination which chooses to defy scripture and embrace apostasy of any kind then the money we sow at that altar joins us with their sin. The act of giving unites us with the perversion and opens the door for the deceptive spirits to infect our entire family. Would anyone with adequate scriptural clarity sow into the destruction of their family? Jesus warned about the proliferation of deception in the last days and we are there. God's intent has always been for the pure corporate (church or ministry) altar to positively influence both the individual and the culture. God established a picture for us when He commanded the Old Testament priests that every offering presented required the salt of the covenant to be acceptable. Jesus picking up on this theme in Mark 9:50 commanded us to ". . . Have salt in yourselves, and have peace with one another." Elijah had salt and demonstrated it by praying the economy closed establishing a confrontation with the proiphets of Baal. Once the perversion was removed, he prayed again and the rain came. Every denomination and ministry that accepts and promotes what God abhors should be prayed shut until they repent! Salt is a preservative and should save from corruption, but when the church loses its salt, it cannot win a society or remove the defiling elements necessary to preserve a nation. The condition of the altar is key to regaining salt.

When the integrity of the corporate altar was corrupted, God always sent correction as a covenant blessing. The correction was not always received, but even in rejection, motivation of heart was visibly made manifest and judgment followed!

Will the real Gehazis please stand up before you get carried out!

Here at the altar
Pure hearts are revealed,
Inner motives exposed
And covenants sealed.

CHAPTER 2

THE COVENANTAL DEVELOPMENT OF THE TITHE

The initial appearance of tithing in scripture is recorded in Genesis 14:17–20 following the first time Abraham has to arm his servants and go to war:

> *And the king of Sodom went out to meet him at the Valley of Shaveh (that is, the King's Valley), after his return from the defeat of Chedorlaomer and the kings who were with him. Then Melchizedek king of Salem brought out bread and wine; he was the priest of God Most High. And he blessed him and said: "Blessed be Abram of God Most High, Possessor of heaven and earth; And blessed be God Most High, Who has delivered your enemies into your hand."*

In the process of the war to recover Lot, his family and all the goods of the city, Abram met Melchizedek, the king of Salem, who brought out bread and wine as a symbol of communion. Abram honored him as the priest of the Most High God in giving ten percent of all that was recovered. The priest blessed Abram. This incident reveals the mechanics of tithing. God blessed Abram with a victory and preservation—of a family member. He responded by giving ten percent of all he had taken. By tithing, Abraham's obedience carried a double blessing for his son Isaac. God saved Isaac from the generational tendency of Abraham, which was fleeing in the face of adversity. In the same circumstances that caused Abram to abandon the Promised Land, Isaac stayed, sowed and God brought a hundredfold return. Abram's covenant brought double blessing to his son. Apparently tithing carries a generational blessing.

Since God is the God of Abraham, Isaac and Jacob, it is in His dealing with these three generations that the picture of the "tithe" emerges painting a specific covenantal purpose. God progressively reveals Himself as a covenant keeper and the covenant He made with Abraham, Isaac, and Jacob is the foundation of all that He will do for man.

Jacob's encounter with God reveals the covenantal promises of tithing. He had stolen the blessing of the first-born from Esau and was forced to leave in fear of his life. Covenantal Christianity began as God's response to the heart cry of two men. After two decades Abram did not think he could have a son. Doubt replaced faith so Abram asked in Genesis 15:8, ". . . how shall I know that I will inherit it?" God's answer was blood covenant. As Jacob was journeying he came to a certain place and laid his head on a stone. He dreamed he saw a ladder whose top went all the way into heaven with angels ascending and descending. He named the place Bethel, the House of God. His response to this vision was

Genesis 28:18–19:

> *Then Jacob rose early in the morning, and took the stone that he had put at his head, set it up as a pillar, and poured oil on top of it. And he called the name of that place Bethel; but the name of that city had been Luz previously.*

Jacob treated the stone like an altar and named it "The House of God." Verses 20–22 record the covenant he made with God outlining the core promises for every tither:

> *Then Jacob made a vow, saying, "If God will be with me, and keep me in this way that I am going, and give me bread to eat and clothing to put on, so that I come back to my father's house in peace, then the LORD shall be my God. And this stone which I have set as a pillar shall be God's house, and of all that You give me I will surely give a tenth to You."*

The covenant of the tithe is emerging with clear elements that were not identified in Genesis 14 when Abram gave his tithe to Melchizedek. From Jacob's declaration we can deduce the essential elements of the tithe are:

1. The tithe brings a covenantal guarantee of God's presence with us much like signing a contract for legal counsel. When we sign a contract with an attorney and pay a retainer he becomes our lawyer dedicated to representing us in whatever dimension we face legal challenges. The covenant of the tithe brings God into relationship with us just as retaining legal counsel. When we tithe, God represents us.
2. The covenant of the tithe brings access to God's ability to direct our steps as He reveals the ultimate purpose and plan for our life. Jacob's plea was that God would keep him in the way

in which he was going, encompassing the issues of purpose, passage and power to accomplish the goal.
3. Tithing opens the door of divine provision. Jacob called for bread to eat and king David said, "I've never seen the righteous forsaken or their seed begging bread. . . ."
4. The fourth promise is clothing and shelter from the adversity of climate. As we approach the end of the age, nature demonstrates increasing hostility against man as we fill the land with iniquity.
5. The fifth and final request was protection from hostile people so that he could return to his father's house in peace. In the battle with radical Islam, dare we walk without this covenant protection which also extends to our children? The tithe brings us into relationship with God in which He promises to be our provision. Promising provision does not mean providing something new and exciting to satisfy every whim. For forty years, the clothing did not wear out as Israel trudged through the wilderness because the covenant—keeping God honored His promises.

These are the primary and foundational covenantal elements of the tithe as revealed in Scripture. All five promises are enough to persuade most people that tithing carries exceptional blessing. Every ministry which receives tithes and offerings has an obligation to declare these five blessings on those who give. Are we declaring?

When Israel emerges from Egypt and goes into the Promised Land, another dimension of understanding is added. Leviticus 27:30 states: "And all the tithe of the land, whether of the seed of the land or of the fruit of the tree, is the LORD'S. It is holy to the LORD." Covenant blessing that comes from God is Holy to Him and demands a response of worship from us. That worshipful response is called a tithe.

Deuteronomy 8:18 adds more depth to that understanding: "And you shall remember the LORD your God, for it is He who gives you power to get wealth, that He may establish His covenant which He swore to your fathers, as it is this day." The covenant of the tithe gives power to prosper in order to confirm a relationship with God. God wants to confirm His relationship with His people in blessing. It would be nice if that were currently the case. Many times throughout scripture the prophets complained about the prosperity of the wicked. God would always redefine prosperity as relationship with Him that brings His power on the scene when needed. In addition, He would remind the prophets that man in his wealth was like a flower in the field, here today and gone tomorrow. It would only be there a short time and then pass away.

We need to remember, it was man who initiated the tithe as a praise and worship for what God had done. As a vow of covenantal relationship, Jacob asked for five things that only God could do. Jacob's tithe depended on God's faithfulness. The tithe was instituted out of a victory that God gave Abram based on covenantal relationship. Though the tithe became mandatory during the season of the law, its core was entirely different. The issue of tithing is the issue of responding in worship and activating God's covenant knowing we have continual access to His Throne. Throughout the history of Israel as a nation the prophets understood the covenant of the tithe as foundational to their success as a country. For Malachi, the problem was affecting the nation and in chapter 3, verse 9, he says, "You are cursed with a curse, For you have robbed Me, Even this whole nation."

There is very little said of tithing in the New Testament, which in my view proves the widespread acceptance of its covenantal foundation and practice throughout the church. Jesus said we should do it in Matthew 23:23b and Hebrews 5:8 proclaims the living Christ still receives them today. Added to this is the preponderance of biblical testimony confirming God as a covenant keeper forever. I find no clear evidence that the covenant of tithe has ever been removed but have a lifetime of experience in God's faithfulness in honoring it. Man instituted the tithe with God and God ratified it into a covenant of provision. Abraham initiated Blood Covenant with his request "to know" God would perform what He promised. Jacob follows in those footsteps with covenant language when he discovers that he has found the "House of God." God has always been a covenant maker and keeper. He ratified Abraham's Covenant with Blood forever and Jacob's Covenant with Salt forever. Numbers 18:19 and 24 declare God's purpose for the tithe and, "it is a covenant of salt forever before the Lord with you and your descendants with you." God's covenants never go defunct!

*Tithing itself
Is a worship decision,
And opens the door
For divine provision.*

CHAPTER 3

THE HALF-TRUTH LIE

Repent therefore and be converted, that your sins may be blotted out, so that times of refreshing may come from the presence of the Lord, And that He may send Jesus Christ, who was preached to you before, whom heaven must receive until the times of restoration of all things, which God has spoken by the mouth of all His holy prophets since the world began.

—Acts 3:19–21

This scripture guarantees Jesus will personally supervise the restoration of the church in the last days, fulfilling every prophetic word ever spoken and recorded by His prophets in the Bible! The church must not only become one without spot, wrinkle, or blemish, but an effective army bringing in a worldwide harvest!

Isaiah spoke of the church as spiritual Israel:

Arise, shine; For your light has come. And the glory of the

Lord is risen upon you. For behold, the darkness shall cover the earth, And deep darkness the people; But the Lord will arise over you, And His glory will be seen upon you.
—Isaiah 60:1–2

Isaiah is prophesying visible manifestations of God's blessing that must be seen as a testimony of His grace!

The Gentiles shall come to your light, and kings to the brightness of your rising. Lift up your eyes all around, and see: they all gather together, they come to you; your sons shall come from afar, and your daughters shall be nursed at your side. ***Then you shall see and become radiant, And your heart shall swell with joy; Because the abundance of the sea shall be turned to you, The wealth of the Gentiles shall come to you.***
—Isaiah 60:3–5

Isaiah prophesied a dramatic transfer of wealth from Satan's control to God's. Has this promise been fulfilled in the restoration of all things?

God's Provision for Harvest

This transfer appears to be a two-edged sword. One edge is a judgment on the materialistic world while the other is God's provision for an end-time harvest, but definitely not for personal promotion or satisfying soulish craving.

In Isaiah 61:6 the Lord says, "You shall eat the riches of the Gentiles, and in their glory you shall boast." Worldly people glory and boast in their wealth. Is the church being prepared for a transfer?

Verse 7 says:

Instead of your shame you shall have double honor, And in-

stead of confusion they shall rejoice in their portion. Therefore in their land they shall possess double. . . .

It appears God is once again giving by promise that which must be possessed. Just like the children of Israel coming out of Egypt had to possess the land of promise, so we must possess our Caanan. God gave it by promise, but it was possessed by anointing, perseverance, courage, wisdom, and obedience.

Not everyone who came out of Egypt made it into Caanan. Many fell by the wayside. It was not God's best for them, but it happened.

The Father wants us to go in and possess what He has promised. Sovereignly, God will move for those He has chosen. He has no accidents. I believe we were born and live in this season because God foreordained our participation in an enormous end-time revival.

The foundation for God's blessing is made possible through covenant. It can only be appropriated and dispensed through covenant.

Malachi 3:8–10 alludes to the foundation of our covenant:

Will a man rob God? Yet you have robbed Me. But you say, "In what way have we robbed You?" In tithes and offerings. You are cursed with a curse, For you have robbed Me, Even this whole nation. Bring all the tithes into the storehouse, That there may be food in My house, And prove Me now in this, Says the Lord of hosts, If I will not open for you the windows of heaven And pour out for you such blessing That there will not be room enough to receive it.

The magnitude of this promise is punctuated by a unique challenge. God had said, "Thou shalt not tempt the Lord thy God," but here He says, "Put Me to the test. Prove Me now in this. I dare you!"

If we tithe, do we have such blessing there is not room enough to contain it? Are the windows of heaven open to us to the degree this passage promises? Are the windows of heaven open to the Body of Christ as a whole? Many of us can point to people who are blessed in measure, but are the windows really open to the extent promised?

God claims the earth and everything in it by right of creation, including the silver, gold, and cattle on a thousand hills. In addition, He reserves the right to do whatever He wants with it. The covenant clearly indicates He wants to bless His people, but we must do our part.

This passage has been interpreted for us in a very traditional way, and every minister who goes to Bible school or seminary usually learns the traditional understanding and preaches it accordingly.

As I began to seek the Lord as to why the windows were not open to the majority of the saints, certain surprising insights began to come. For the first time, I saw impurity and manipulation in our traditional way of preaching the tithe. Our first error of tradition was in emphasizing a half-truth. Historically, we emphasized a believer's decision to tithe as the determinate factor guaranteeing God will open the windows of heaven.

Preaching a Half-Truth

We generally preached it this way: "If you will make the decision to tithe, God will open the windows of heaven for you." We placed the entire responsibility on each believer to activate the covenant. By saying, "If you will tithe, God will open the windows of heaven," we preached a half-truth, because there is more involved. A half-truth can quickly degenerate into untruth.

The other side of the coin would say, "If the windows are

not open, the fault is with you!" The scenario has unfolded progressively. We preach, "If you tithe, God will . . . ," but God has not in measure promised; therefore, where are we missing God's promises? How do we explain the windows still not being open for those who have faithfully tithed?

Perhaps a portion of the answer is in a more comprehensive understanding of covenant. Marriage is an example of covenant. No one can marry himself. A covenant is a mutual agreement between two separate parties. You cannot have a covenant unless two individuals agree.

The language of Malachi 3 speaks of covenant. When two people come to terms in covenant, and as each diligently adheres to those terms, the agreement is consummated. Why get married and not consummate the covenant? God has offered a fundamental monetary covenant to His people, but it is obvious from the financial condition of the saints that the covenant is not being fully consummated. How long would a marriage last in that condition?

In nearly every congregation, the majority of people who tithe will agree, "We tithe and are doing the best we know to do, but we do not see the windows of heaven opened to the full extent God promised." The real question is, why? Assuming it is not God's fault, we must ask ourselves, "Where are we missing it?"

Jesus referred to a potential answer when He said in Mark 7:13, "Your traditions have made the word of God of none effect." Is it possible our teaching of the tithe in the traditional way, as we learned it in Bible school, has made the Word of God of none effect, closing rather than opening the windows of heaven? I believe this is one of several root causes.

Jesus clearly exposed our first tradition in Matthew 23:13–19, when He said:

But woe to you, scribes and Pharisees, hypocrites. For you

shut up *the kingdom of heaven against men; for you neither go in yourselves, nor do you allow those who are entering to go in. Woe to you, scribes and Pharisees, hypocrites. For you devour widows' houses, and for a pretense make long prayers. Therefore you will receive greater condemnation. Woe to you, scribes and Pharisees, hypocrites. For you travel land and sea to win one proselyte, and when he is won, you make him twice as much a son of hell as yourselves. Woe to you, blind guides, who say, "Whoever swears by the temple, it is nothing; but whoever swears by the gold of the temple, he is obliged to perform it." Fools and blind. For which is greater, the gold or the temple that sanctifies the gold? And, "Whoever swears by the altar, it is nothing; but whoever swears by the gift that is on it, he is obliged to perform it." Fools and blind. For which is greater,* **the gift** *or* **the altar** *that sanctifies the gift?*

In our traditional teaching of the tithe, we have made the gift greater than the altar which sanctifies the gift. We can no longer assume the altar sanctifies the gift without checking on biblical foundation.

By preaching the tithe in the traditional way, we have been able to build a steady financial base in our local churches without any obligation on our part to organizationally adhere to God's revealed plan. This gives leadership the freedom to do what they want to do, and places all the burden on the saints.

The fruit of our tradition is everywhere in manifestation. There is a distinct lack of open windows to God's people who tithe. There has been a measure of blessing, but it is probably based more on grace than obedience.

Which is greater, the gift or the altar that sanctifies the gift? Jesus said those of us who thought the gift was greater than the altar are fools and blind. According to Jesus, *the condition of the place where we give is more important than the giving.*

The Greek word translated "sanctify" is **hag-ee-ad-zo**. It means "to make, render or declare, sacred or holy, to consecrate." This word appears in The Lord's Prayer, "Hallowed be thy name. . . ." It is translated in a number of places "sanctify, or sanctified." **Hag-ee-adzo** appears in Acts 20:32 in a context similar to Matthew 23.

> *And now, brethren, I commend you to God and to the word of His grace, which is able to build you up and give you an inheritance among all those who are sanctified.*

Hag-ee-ad-zo here, as in Matthew 23, means, "to separate from things profane and dedicate to God, to consecrate and so render inviolable."

When a monetary gift is put on a pure altar, it is made holy and acceptable to God; consequently, the covenant is completed. But the converse of that is also true. When the gift or tithe is put on an impure altar, it is made unholy, and the covenant is not completed.

We have failed to understand a foundational principle: The purity of the altar *sanctifies* the gift. The condition of the altar determines the return on the giving both temporal and eternal. This is why Jesus started out by saying to the Pharisees, "You shut up the kingdom of heaven against men." How many of us as leaders today are guilty of shutting the windows of heaven to the saints by tradition without realizing it? We will answer for that in eternity.

Jesus intimates the purity of the altar is more important than the money placed on it by saying, "Which is greater, the gift or the altar that sanctifies the gift?" For this covenant to be complete, each side must do its part to consummate the contract.

It is much more advantageous for those in leadership who want to do their own thing to emphasize the tithe without ever mentioning the condition of the altar. This mindset leaves the leader free to do whatever seems good financially. But the fruit of the system is seen in the condition of the victims. The windows of heaven for many people seem closed. The context of Matthew 23 makes it very clear; Jesus is speaking about covenantal giving:

> *Woe to you, scribes and Pharisees, hypocrites. For you pay tithe of mint and anise and cummin, and have neglected the weightier matters of the law: justice and mercy and faith. These you ought to have done, without leaving the others undone.*

What churches today neglect the weightier matters of the Word and refuse to proclaim a standard of holiness in an attempt to gain more members? Seeker-sensitive Christianity has to prosper by volume because it cannot sanctify what the people give. We have no grounds for complaint about financial provision if we put our tithes on the altar of half-hearted Christianity.

Jesus told them they had emphasized the tithe while neglecting other principles which ultimately affect the tithe. In effect, He said, "You have made the gift greater than the altar which sanctifies the gift, allowing you to do what you want financially but leaving people impoverished." This passage perfectly describes some of the fruit we have in Christendom today.

This understanding requires we deal with a variety of questions:

- What transpires in the realm of the spirit when we do business with God at an impure altar?
- What effect does the impurity have on the covenant?
- What makes an altar impure?
- How can we recognize an impure altar?

- What should we do to restore purity if, in fact, we discover the altar where we attend is impure?

In Scripture, the altar was a place where man was led to do business with God; a place where God spoke to him and he responded with commitment. The altar was a place where the purpose and plan of God was received with commitment and dedication of heart.

The Old Testament altar and what transpired there is in many ways a type and shadow of the business we should do with God in our New Testament churches. When we look at the purity of the altar, we are dealing with the purity of the local church.

1 Kings, chapters 12 and 13, give one example of impurity at the altar. God had spoken to Solomon about judgment as a result of his disobedience. But because of his father, David, Solomon would not see the judgment in his days; it would be deferred to his son's days.

Two Kingdoms

First Kings 12 is the account of Rehoboam, Solomon's son, taking charge of Israel, and God raising up an enemy named Jeroboam to fulfill the prophecy by taking ten of the twelve tribes, leaving Rehoboam with two.

Jeroboam's kingdom and the ten tribes became known as Israel, or the Northern Kingdom, and Rehoboam's two tribes became known as Judah, or the Southern Kingdom. The spirit of fear came on Jeroboam to move him beyond what God had commanded.

Then Jeroboam built Shechem in the mountains of Ephraim, and dwelt there. Also he went out from there and built Penuel. And Jeroboam said in his heart, "Now the kingdom may return to the house of David [fear]: "If these people go up to offer sacrifices in the house of the Lord at Jerusalem, then the heart of this people will turn back to their lord, Rehoboam king of Judah, and they will kill me and go back to Rehoboam king of Judah." Therefore the king took counsel and made two calves of gold, and said to the people, "It is too much for you to go up to Jerusalem. Here are your gods, O Israel, which brought you up from the land of Egypt!" And he set up one in Bethel, and the other he put in Dan. Now this thing became a sin, for the people went to worship before the one as far as Dan.

—1 Kngs 12:25–30

Jeroboam was afraid to let the Israelites go back to Jerusalem to worship. He was afraid he would lose *control.* In his mind, the only way to keep what God had given was to start his own church. God had not commanded him to do that. First Kings 12:31–32 states:

He made shrines on the high places, and made priests from every class of people, who were **not of the sons of Levi.** *Jeroboam ordained a feast on the fifteenth day of the eighth month,* **like the feast that was in Judah***, and offered sacrifices on the altar. So he did at Bethel, sacrificing to the calves that he had made. And at Bethel he installed the priests of the high places which* **he had made.**

In order to keep his own denomination going, Jeroboam had to recruit priests, once again departing from God's ordained plan. According to verse 32, he did his best to duplicate the same meeting days and form of worship God had set up for His people in Jerusalem.

A very interesting phrase begins to appear in verses 32 and 33. It is the phrase "he had made." It appears three times, and distinctively points out the difference between man doing something because he wants to, versus waiting and letting God fulfill the divine plan. Verse 33 reveals the true foundation of this altar:

> *So he made offerings on the altar which **he had made** at Bethel on the fifteenth day of the eighth month, in the month which **he had devised** in his own heart. And he ordained a feast for the children of Israel, and offered sacrifices on the altar and burned incense.*

One of the ingredients which makes an altar pure or impure is the motivation of the individual who sets it up. Did God ordain the ministry or was it devised out of man's heart? How much of what is done there is from God, and how much is from man? What is the motivation for what is done, who is brought in, and what is preached? God's response toward impure altars is given in chapter 13:1–2:

> *And behold, a man of God went from Judah to Bethel by the word of the Lord, and Jeroboam stood by the altar to burn incense. Then he cried out against the altar by the word of the Lord, and said, "O altar, altar. Thus says the Lord: 'Behold, a child, Josiah by name, shall be born to the house of David; and on you he shall sacrifice the priests of the high places who burn incense on you, and men's bones shall be burned on you.'"*

The first law of the impure altar states that when a man devises in his own heart and raises up a ministry God has not ordained, he will die on the very altar he builds. Seasons of this judgment usually fall in every generation. Spiritual death is far worse than physical death. In spiritual death, you watch another move in the anointing you once had. First Kings 13:3 is very distinctive in that it shows the ashes poured out or going down. In some instances, when sacrifices were offered on the altar and accepted by God, the fire fell from heaven, the aroma ascended to God, and it was accepted.

At an impure altar, instead of being accepted, the ashes are poured out or rejected. When we tithe into an impure altar, it is like pouring money into a hole. God is in no way obligated to bring the promised return, and the windows of heaven remain closed.

Impure altars never go unchallenged. The prophet came to speak the word of the Lord against the impurity of the altar, and the war was on. Jeroboam would much rather destroy the prophet than repent and destroy the altar. That attitude is still prevalent today revealing hardness of heart.

When the king receives judgment in his own body as a reward for trying to destroy the prophet, it immediately changes his attitude. He wants his hand restored, so he asks the prophet to pray. When his hand is restored, the king asks the man of God to come home, promising to bless him and feed him, but the man of God says:

> *If you were to give me half your house, I would not go in with you; nor would I eat bread or drink water in this place. For so it was commanded me by the word of the Lord, saying, "You shall not eat bread, nor drink water, nor return by the same way you came."*
>
> —1 Kings 13:8–9

This speaks of a spiritual truth which is working whether we know it or not. Eating bread and drinking water is, of course, a type and shadow of the spiritual bread and heavenly refreshing of the anointing which we desperately need in our lives. Its effect is to transform us as we receive from a pure altar. But when we participate in an impure altar, we receive something entirely different.

The anointing imparted at a pure altar brings growth, maturity, and blessing, but the anointing imparted at an impure altar brings corruption and eventually various levels of destruction. When God commanded the prophet not to eat or drink in that place, He sent a clear message about the impact of impure altars. The impurity is reproduced in all who partake. God commands the prophet to eat no bread and drink no water in that place. What is God commanding us? What condition is the place where we are spiritually eating and drinking? Are we spiritually starved? The proof is in the pudding!

Identifying With an Altar

Giving either tithe or offering fully and totally identifies us with the altar. By sowing seed into an altar, we are identified with that altar, for good and blessing or hurt and destruction!

> *He who receives a prophet in the name of a prophet shall receive a prophet's reward.*
> —Matthew 10:41

If we are giving into an altar of impurity, that impurity is transferred to us, and if we are giving to a pure altar, that purity becomes part of us. Jeroboam was very smart. He did not go to an out-of-the-way, unusual place, but to one that was acceptable, well known, and respected by people. Bethel was one place where God's house historically stayed.

This is a perfect example of how the devil operates today. Where does he work through deception to bring impurity? In the place where we all attend and know that God has ordained for us to grow and develop. The main attack is against the church.

The greatest gift God gave man was creation in His likeness, with the ability to procreate eternal beings. The Old Testament confirms this view in several ways. If a man took a wife and he died having no children, it was the responsibility of the next youngest brother to marry her and raise up children. Deuteronomy 25:5–10 makes it very clear that God demanded brothers to take this issue very seriously.

Genesis 38 records Judah having a firstborn son named Er, who took a wife named Tamar. Er died and Judah commanded Onan (Er's younger brother) to take Tamar and raise up children for Er. Genesis 38:9–10 states, "But Onan knew that the heir would not be his; and it came to pass, when he went in to his brother's wife, that he emitted on the ground, lest he should give an heir to his brother. And the thing which he did displeased the LORD; therefore He killed him also." The gift of creating eternal beings was valued to the point of severely judging those who refused and rejected the gift. God killed Onan!

The greatest grief a parent has is losing a child, but closely following that is discovering a child rejects the gift of raising up future generations for the substitute of self-gratification with a same-sex partner. Some of the most wonderfully gifted and loving people make this devastating choice. What is the church to do? On one side, we have the great commission demanding we make disciples of all nations encouraging us to witness and win the homosexual. On the other side, we have clear scriptural mandates like Leviticus 20:22–24 declaring statutorily protecting homosexuality fills the land with iniquity and deprives the people of the ability to defend themselves.

If we choose to protect homosexuality, we lose our nation. While standing against the homosexual agenda nationally, we still have the obligation to love the individual and confront their lifestyle choice in the hope of repentance and salvation. If as church policy we choose to bless same-sex unions, then Acts 20:26–27 destroys us on Judgment Day. It says, "Therefore I testify to you this day that I am innocent of the blood of all men. For I have not shunned to declare to you the whole counsel of God." Can you imagine becoming personally responsible for the loss in eternity of homosexual friends because we bless behavior that God clearly declares disqualifies from salvation? First Corinthians 6:9–11 both warns and encourages our ministry to homosexuals:

> *Do you not know that the unrighteous will not inherit the kingdom of God? Do not be deceived. Neither fornicators, nor idolaters, nor adulterers, nor homosexuals, nor sodomites, nor thieves, nor covetous, nor drunkards, nor revilers, nor extortioners will inherit the kingdom of God. And such were some of you. But you were washed, but you were sanctified, but you were justified in the name of the Lord Jesus and by the Spirit of our God.*

Verse 9 warns about eternally disqualifying behavior, but verse 11 encourages us about an anointing that delivers a person from a perverted sexual orientation. The early church apparently had a significant number of individuals delivered from homosexuality. For those of us who believe in the inerrancy of Scripture, this should settle the issue. If we choose as a ministry or church to reject God's Word and bless same-sex unions, we invite a spirit of perversion as an idol to dominate the altar. All who give there can develop the same deception. By giving to such an altar, we can bring ourselves under the same God-appointed judgment due the altar. If we bless when God demands we lovingly confront, the Ananias and Sapphira events in the future may be ours for lying about God!

Deliverance from homosexuality like anything else begins with God's Word: ". . . but such were some of you . . ." reveals homosexuality to be a personal choice. God has never created anyone homosexual. Refusing to accept God's Word on the personal choice destroys any hope of deliverance. The power of the gospel is in what happens when a person chooses to believe through the foolishness of preaching. The Word is powerful, but must be **received and believed** to manifest. Demons work hard to destroy the preaching of the Word.

Suppose we find ourselves in a church structure choosing to accept and bless homosexuality where a homosexual has been ordained as a bishop. Even though our congregation may disagree, the portion of Parish money sent to the national organization ties us to an apostate altar. The spirit of homosexuality now has access to our entire family because of our giving. We gave to an impure altar and the same spirit of deception blinding the homosexual has judicial access to eat our family alive. Why do we open doors to deceptive spirits? Stop supporting impurity at the altar. Our children will thank us throughout eternity.

A biblical example of what can happen to us if we refuse to confront and separate from such sin is the old prophet at Bethel. An old prophet who had been living in Bethel came out to talk to the young prophet and tried to persuade him to come to his house for fellowship. The young prophet repeated the word of the Lord in verses 16–18:

> *And he said, "I cannot return with you nor go in with you; neither can I eat bread or drink water with you in this place. "For I have been told by the word of the Lord, 'You shall not eat bread nor drink water there, nor return by going the way you came.'" He said to him, "I too am a prophet as you are, and an angel spoke to me by the word of the Lord, saying, 'Bring him back with you to your house, that he may eat bread and drink water.'" But he lied to him.*

How can a minister lie using prophesy? Using prophecy to manipulate people to our own ends will end in judgment. Only a seared conscience could do such a thing. Could the fruit of an impure altar produce a seared conscience? It seems to have here. The young prophet went back and ate bread and drank water with the old prophet at Bethel. Verses 21 and 22 are even more revealing. The old prophet now speaks the authentic word of the Lord to the young prophet:

> . . . *Because you have disobeyed the word of the Lord, and have not kept the commandment which the Lord your God commanded you, but you came back, ate bread, and drank water in the place of which the Lord said to you, "Eat no bread and drink no water," your corpse shall not come to the tomb of your fathers.*

Impure altars produce spiritual corpses. The young prophet left for home. He was met by a lion and immediately killed. The lion stood there without moving; neither did it eat the body. This was a sign to the religious people that the spoken word of the Lord had been and would be fulfilled. Why do we support impure altars that, like the lion, take our spiritual life? The first time I ever read this passage, I thought, "God, that is not fair." But sometimes in our humanistic society we need to remember God's Kingdom operates on obedience.

I began to question how an old prophet could out of one side of his mouth lie convincingly and yet, just a few hours later, out of the other side of the same mouth, speak the word of the Lord. What turned the old prophet into an impure vessel spewing mixed seed?

An Impure Prophet

Undoubtedly, the old prophet became like the altar at which he worshipped. He lived at Bethel. Was he a prophet? Yes, he was, but instead of moving to a pure altar, he stayed at a place where there was impurity. This produced mixed seed in his own life. On Judgment Day, he will give account for the life of the young prophet.

This should speak to us about the reason why we go where we go to church. Is it close? Is it conveniently located? Can we really afford decisions based on convenience? When we look at the eternal repercussions, convenience is absolutely the worse reason for going to a church and can, in fact, be the very leverage Satan uses to bring mixed seed into our lives. A little convenience here may breed a great deal of inconvenience throughout eternity. The law of the altar states, *the condition of the altar where you attend, participate, and put your money is reproduced in your life, whether you are aware of it or not.* It is a spiritual law.

The old prophet could speak the word of the Lord, but because he had for a long time been in a place of impurity, he could *also* lie convincingly to get what he wanted. It was the same spirit which built the altar to start with. The lawlessness and willingness of Jeroboam to do whatever necessary to insure keeping what he wanted was transferred to the old prophet. Selfish ambition, which draws Jeroboam to build the altar, begins to reign as a ruling spirit over this altar, permeating those who come to worship. The old prophet, moving in this spirit, stole the life of the young prophet.

What transpires at an altar should bring covenantal blessing, but in some cases, it brings a curse. Discerning mixed seed can be a challenge. Acts 20:25–28 enumerates an oft-violated principle in today's seeker-friendly environment:

> *And indeed, now I know that you all, among whom I have gone preaching the kingdom of God, will see my face no*

> *more. Therefore I testify to you this day that I am innocent of the blood of all men. For I have not shunned to declare to you the whole counsel of God. Therefore take heed to yourselves and to all the flock, among which the Holy Spirit has made you overseers, to shepherd the church of God which He purchased with His own blood.*

Any minister who knowingly omits sections of God's Word because it may be too offensive to the flesh, the culture or the politically correct will find blood on his hands and be utterly speechless on Judgment Day. Is there any difference between what Jeroboam did in building his ministry and what is routinely done today? Both ministry philosophies embraced the same foundational pillars. The problem with what Jeroboam built was "he made it." When ministers knowingly choose to delete a portion of the whole counsel and preach and practice only what is palatable to the masses, how can we call it anything but mixed seed? The fruit of mixed seed would be a lack of discernment in the people because of the deficit of God's Word. Flee such an altar before the men who started it die on it.

The moral of this impure altar is that it cost a young leader of the next generation his life. The text is very deliberate to delineate the difference between the young prophet and the old prophet. The mixed seed of the old prophet cost the young prophet his life. Mixed seed altars are convenient and inviting, but ultimately cost us a generation of leaders destroyed by disobedience. Flee for your life before the deception deepens into detrimental damage or demise!

Have you ever considered that covenantal principles which dictate giving could bring a curse instead of a blessing? In Malachi 2:1–2 God demands the priests honor His commandments. He promises to those who refuse that He will "curse" their "blessings." Keil and Delitzsch, a bastion of conservative scholarship, state in Volume 10 pages 442–443,[2] "If they shall not do this, God will send the curse, against them, and that in two ways. In the first place, He will curse their blessings; in fact, He has already done so. *Berakhoth*, blessings, are obviously not the revenues of the priests, tithes, atonement-money, and portions of the sacrifices (L. de Dieu, Ros., Hitzig), but the blessings pronounced by the priests upon the people by virtue of their office. These God will curse, i.e., He will make them ineffective, or turn them into the very opposite."

Is it possible to write a check on Sunday morning and have God turn the prayer of blessing into a judgment of destruction? The condition of the altar determines blessing or curse. If the altar where we attend is defiled, defilement enters our life because sowing into it makes us "one with it." The defilement we support will slowly grow into acceptance transforming how we think and act. When we uphold what God Abhors and refuse to repent, judgment is inevitable.

The enemy through tradition has defiled many altars. We can have a pure heart but be operating in tradition, and the enemy has joined us with that altar to stop the covenant blessing. He is a legalist accomplishing his goal through deception.

If we tithe and the windows of heaven are not open to us, then it is time to ask the Lord to show us any areas of impurity, either personally or corporately, so that we can take appropriate action.

---

2. *Commentary on the Old Testament, Vol. 10*, pp. 442–443 , C.F. Keil and F. Delitzsch, William B. Eerdmans Publishing Company, Grand Rapids, MI.

*We need to stay watchful
And keep our hearts humble,
For our old traditions
May cause us to stumble.*

*There is more to tithing
We may not quite see,
The altar we "bow" to
Where is its purity?*

CHAPTER 4

COVENANT-DESTROYING TRADITION

The second major tradition causing impurity at the altar comes from the traditional way we teach tithing. We teach Malachi 3:8–10 as a *distribution* passage, when it really is a *purpose* passage. "Bring all the tithes into the storehouse, That there may be meat in My house."

We, by tradition, have emphasized, "Bring all the tithes into the storehouse" because it suits our purpose without honoring the obligation to fulfill "That there may be meat in My house." We have preached, "Bring the tithe here," while glossing over the real intent of this scripture. God is quite specific about the ones to whom He gave the tithe. Misleading God's people brings impurity to the altar, especially when done with a motivation for self-gain. Numbers 18 is one of the distribution passages, and verses 19 through 22 show clearly God's intent for the tithe:

]All the heave offerings of the holy things, which the children of Israel offer to the Lord, **I have given to you** *and your sons and daughters with you as an ordinance forever; it is a covenant of salt forever before the Lord with you and your descendants with you. The Lord said to Aaron: "You shall have no inheritance in their land, nor shall you have any portion among them; I am your portion and your inheritance among the children of Israel. Behold, I have given the* **children of Levi** *all the tithes in Israel as an inheritance in return for the work which they perform, the work of the tabernacle of meeting. Hereafter the children of Israel shall not come near the tabernacle of meeting, lest they bear sin and die."*

The Scripture does not say God gave the tithe to the local synagogue, as we have traditionally preached. He gave it to the Levites and immediately added, "You had better not assume a Levitical position, lest you die."

God certainly knows human nature as it relates to money. He knows the heart of man, and acts accordingly. God gave the tithe to the Levites and admonished the people not to assume a Levitical position for financial reasons. With great persecution plaguing the early church, there was no incentive to start a church unless divinely called. In most nations, the same hostile environment prevails. As Islam increases in nations, so does the martyrdom of the church.

As long as we continue to affirm the notion that the tithe belongs to the storehouse, those who are not called will start them in nations with no persecution.

False Pastors

The fruit of our tradition has been, in some cases, people who are neither gifted nor called to five-fold positions establishing churches for the wrong reason. The traditional understanding of the tithe entices individuals to step out of their God-ordained gifting and calling to "pastor" individually.

We have, in the church world today, quite a variety of one-man shows. Many who are pastoring are, in fact, gifted and called to other areas. Some feel compelled to do so in order to obtain a paycheck and support their families. In effect, through tradition, we have institutionalized a traditional understanding of the tithe and in the process have destroyed the very covenant foundation for God's intended blessing in our lives.

God *did* say to bring the tithe into the storehouse, but when does a ministry qualify as a Bible storehouse, and when does it not? We assume just because a sign out front says "XYZ Church Services Sunday 10 a.m. and 6 p.m." that it is a storehouse. Nothing could be further from the truth. Nowhere in the New Testament is *one* man pointed to as the "pastor." Shepherding was a recognized function of the elders, who were called and gifted by God in at least five major areas.

The Bible guarantees judgment and removal when people assume positions because of wrong motivation. God always gives a season of grace in which to discern, repent, and obey.

Numbers 18:23–24 says:

But the Levites shall perform the work of the tabernacle of meeting, and they shall bear their iniquity; it shall be a statute forever, throughout your generations, that among the children of Israel they shall have no inheritance. For the tithes of the children of Israel, which they offer up as a heave offering to the Lord, I have given to the Levites. . . .

What was the purpose of giving the tithe to the Levites? In Malachi 3, it was "That there may be meat in My house." Second

Chronicles 31:4–5 is very distinctive in its application, as it fully corroborates Malachi 3 in decreeing the purpose for the tithe:

> *Moreover he commanded the people who dwelt in Jerusalem to contribute support for the priests and the Levites, that they might **devote themselves to the Law of the Lord**. As soon as the commandment was circulated, the children of Israel brought in abundance the firstfruits of grain and wine, oil and honey, and of all the produce of the field; and they brought in abundantly the **tithe** of everything.*

The scripture is clear and consistent. In Numbers 18, 2 Chronicles 31, and Malachi 3, the stated purpose of the tithe is to support the Levites, plural not singular. It was given to the Levites, through the storehouse, so they might devote themselves to the word of the Lord and bring the meat of the Word to God's people, causing growth and maturity. But who are the Levites?

The answer to that question lies in understanding types and shadows of the three priesthoods in the Old Testament. From highest to lowest they are: Melchizedek, Aaron, and the Levites. Melchizedek was a type and shadow of the eternal ministry of the Lord Jesus Christ according to Hebrews 7.

Hebrews 7:4–11 says:

> *Now consider how great this man was [Melchizedek], to whom even the patriarch Abraham gave a tenth of the spoils. And indeed those who are of the sons of Levi, who receive the priesthood, have a commandment to receive tithes from the people according to the law, that is, from their brethren, though they have come from the loins of Abraham; but he [Melchizedek] whose genealogy is not derived from them received tithes from Abraham and blessed him who had the promises.*

Abraham, in obedience to God, instituted the tithe long before the law ever came into being. The covenant of the tithe transcends the law and is still in force today!

> *Now beyond all contradiction the lesser is blessed by the better. Here mortal men receive tithes, **but there he receives them**, of whom it is witnessed that **he** [Jesus] **lives**. Even Levi, who receives tithes, paid tithes through Abraham, so to speak, for he was still in the loins of his father when Melchizedek met him. Therefore, if perfection were through the Levitical priesthood (for under it the people received the law), what further need was there that another priest should rise according to the order of Melchizedek, and **not be called** according to the order of Aaron?*

Aaron's high priesthood was, in many ways, a type and shadow of Jesus' ministry, but in one major way was not, while Melchizedek's was, according to Hebrews 7. Aaron's priesthood was temporal; it would end at his death and must be passed to another. Melchizedek, without father or mother, was a type of the eternal King-Priest Jesus, whose ministry will never pass away. In some ways, Aaron has done double-duty because he represents (as a type and shadow) aspects of both Christ's ministry and the New Testament believers. Consequently, Jesus is called ". . . the firstborn among many brethren."

In what way did God consider all His saints in the New Covenant and say, "You have an Aaronic ministry?" What did Aaron do that was prophetic of the believer? He personally went into the Holy of Holies once a year.

Matthew 27:51 records at the death of Jesus that the veil of the Temple was torn in two, from top to bottom, as a sign that the price had been paid for all to come before the Father. Suddenly, for the first time, the way was open for all the people to come before the Lord. Hebrews 9:8 puts it this way:

> . . . the Holy Spirit indicating this, that the way into the Holiest of All was not yet made manifest while the first tabernacle was still standing.

What only Aaron, the High Priest, could do once a year in coming into God's presence in Old Testament times has now been made possible for all New Testament believers to do daily.

The Levitical Ministry

We can go into the presence of God, offer sacrifices of praise, and make intercession for sinners according to God's perfect will and plan. In many ways, Aaron is a type and shadow of the New Testament believer. But who, then, are the Levites (the third and lowest form of priesthood in the Old Testament)?

Numbers 8:13–19 gives valuable insight into the Levitical ministry:

> *And you shall stand the Levites before Aaron and his sons, and then offer them as though a wave offering to the Lord. Thus you shall separate the Levites from among the children of Israel, and the Levites shall be Mine. After that the Levites shall go in to service the tabernacle of meeting. So you shall cleanse them and offer them, as though a wave offering. For they are wholly given to Me from among the children of Israel; I have taken them for Myself instead of all who open the womb, the firstborn of all the children of Israel. For all the firstborn among the children of Israel are Mine, both man and beast; on the day that I struck all the firstborn in the land of Egypt I sanctified them to Myself. I have taken*

the Levites instead of all the firstborn of the children of Israel. I have given the Levites as a gift to Aaron and his sons from among the children of Israel, to do the work for the children of Israel in the tabernacle of meeting, and to make atonement for the children of Israel. . . .

Three corresponding scriptures have "thats" which fit together, contributing to our accurate understanding of the tithe. Malachi 3:10 says, "Bring the tithes into the storehouse **that**, there may be meat in My house."

Second Chronicles 31:4 says, ". . . **that** the Levites may devote themselves to the word of the Lord."

Numbers 8:19 says, ". . . **that** there be no plague among the children of Israel when the children of Israel come near. . . ."

The Levites were to mature the believers by teaching God's Word. They were to make people aware of God's requirements so that no plague fell upon the people when coming near God. The Levites were charged with preparing people to fulfill covenant purposes through understanding God's Word.

Who are the New Testament Levites? Verse 19 says they were given as "gifts to Aaron." Ephesians 4:7–11 also speaks of gifts given to New Testament Aarons.

*But to each one of us grace was given according to the measure of Christ's gift. Therefore He says: "When He ascended on high, He led captivity captive, And gave gifts to men." [Now this, "He ascended"—what does it mean but that He also descended into the lower parts of the earth? He who descended is also the One who ascended far above all the heavens, that He might fill all things.] And He Himself gave some to be **apostles**, some **prophets**, some **evangelists**, and some **pastors**, and **teachers**. . . .*

Who are the New Testament Levites? They are the apostles, prophets, evangelists, pastors, and teachers. Is the purpose of this New Testament Levitical ministry the same as that of the Old Testament Levites?

Ephesians 4:12 tells us:

> *. . . for the equipping of the saints for the working of ministry, for the edifying of the body of Christ, till we all come to the unity of the faith and the knowledge of the Son of God, to a perfect* [or mature] *man, to the measure of the stature of the fullness of Christ; that we should no longer be children, tossed to and fro and carried about with every wind of doctrine, by the trickery of men, in the cunning craftiness by which they lie in wait to deceive. . . .*

It appears the same purpose is stated here, but in slightly different language. The Old Testament Levites and New Testament fivefold are both called **gifts**. They both have the purpose of maturing the saints by bringing forth meat. Both contribute to helping people walk in a way pleasing to God through the fullness of His covenant, ensuring there will be no plague or deception among God's people. The purpose is basically the same. When preaching the tithe, we said, "If you tithe, God will open the windows of heaven to you." This left people with a half-truth.

A number of years ago, I was going home from what in all outward appearances was a great meeting. The anointing was strong on the teaching, and God moved in various gifts of the Spirit, but I could not shake inner dissatisfaction. By all the standard criteria, it was a dynamite meeting, but in my spirit there was something missing.

As I asked the Lord what was wrong, the Holy Spirit said, "Son, it is not what you told them that is the problem. What was said was true and good. It is what you did *not* tell them that will get them in trouble." The Bible presents truth in tension: grace *vs.* justice, mercy *vs.* judgment, healing *vs.* suffering, deliverance *vs.* adversity in trials that mature and Armenianism *vs.* Calvinism. Hebrew culture holds truth in tension while Western minds want truth concrete. I realized it was not enough to bring forth a measure of truth in a service.

There is a tendency at times when we have a teaching ministry to consistently trumpet one God-given evaluation until the church is in the ditch. In the early years of the Charismatic renewal, faith was taught without the cross, creating a rather large Armenian ditch. Keep yourself in the center of God's will by purposing to hold truth in tension. It is the job of the Holy Spirit to navigate us through each tension. One morning, He may witness in our hearts to "wait on the Lord" (Calvinistic) while the following morning witnessing to act or take a step (Armenian). The Christian life is one of allowing the Holy Spirit to lead us through the tensions of truth demonstrating God is GOD and we are not!

A New Accountability

The Lord was calling me to a new accountability in measuring out the truth and bringing it forth fully balanced so people would not run with part of the answer and end up consistently in misapplication. God holds teachers to a higher standard. James 3 says the teaching ministry has the greatest accountability of all.

In Matthew 23:16–19, as Jesus dealt with hypocrisy; He confronted the scribes and Pharisees and rebuked the entire religious system:

> *Woe to you, blind guides, who say, "Whoever swears by the temple, it is nothing; but whoever swears by the gold of the temple, he is obliged to perform it." Fools and blind. For*

which is greater, the gold or the temple that sanctifies the gold? And, "whoever swears by the altar, it is nothing; but whoever swears by the gift that is on it, he is obliged to perform it." Fools and blind. For which is greater, the gift or the altar that sanctifies the gift?

We did in our preaching what we learned in Bible school and made the gift more important than the altar. It is not what we told people that got them in trouble, but what we did not tell them. We did *not* tell them because we did not know how to discern impure altars.

Jesus made one thing clear: It is not your tithe and offering in itself which makes the covenant work. What makes the covenant work is the union of God's purpose, an individual's obedient heart with purity in the altar where they give their tithe. Purity completes the covenant and guarantees fulfilled promises.

The condition of the altar either makes the tithe holy or unholy, pure or impure, accepted or rejected. When you put tithe or offering on an impure altar, you lose your covenant promise for God's multiplication and increase. God is not obligated, because the money is not sanctified. A perfect example of how the enemy has attacked the church is seen in Joshua 6, where Israel was beginning to possess the Promised Land. They could not talk or say a word for seven long days. God was teaching them obedience!

"The Tithe Is Mine"

Jericho was the only city where God said, "You cannot have any of the spoil. It all belongs to Me." Jericho became a type of the tithe, or first ten percent. In every other city, God said, "The spoil is yours." But in the very first city He said, "It is mine. Do not touch it." The two Hebrew words used to describe the spoil of Jericho are **kheh-rem** and **khaw-ram**.

In the Lexical Aids to the Old Testament section of *The Hebrew Greek Key Study Bible*,[3] **kheh-rem** is described as follows:

It was an object. The essential meaning is "forbidden" or "prohibited" which was surrendered to God into His service or something declared for utter destruction. The most famous example was the entire city of Jericho and everything in it (Joshua 6:17).

Everything flammable was to be burned or reserved for God. However, Achan took some things which were in the city. This caused the whole nation of Israel to be affected by the violation.

They lost an easy battle at Ai (Joshua 7:12-13). Sin was in the camp and it had to be removed before God would make them victorious again. Jericho was a pagan city which defiantly opposed God's work. *Through Achan, Israel unwittingly became associated with Jericho.*

The Hebrew root word for **kheh-rem** is **khaw-ram**. Lexical Aids to the Old Testament says, "The basic idea was that of setting something aside strictly for God's use. It was considered most holy by God, and therefore could not be sold or redeemed by any substitutionary measure."

It is clear from studying these words that they carry two basic ideas: (1) they described items to be surrendered or given over to God, and (2) they implied both the blessing for obedience and a curse for disobedience, which is also part of the covenant language used in Malachi 3.

Interestingly enough, the same two Hebrew words are used to describe the tithe as "devoted or holy" to the Lord in Leviticus 27:28–30:

---

3. *The Hebrew Greek Key Study Bible, Lexical Aids to the Old Testament,* King James Version, Compiler and Editor Spiros Zodhiates, Baker Book House, Grand Rapids, MI 49506. Copyright 1984, p. 2764.

Nevertheless no devoted [kheh-rem] *offering that a man may devote* [kheh-rem] *to the Lord of all that he has, both man and beast, or the field of his possession, shall be sold or redeemed; every devoted* [kheh-rem] *offering is most holy to the Lord. No person* [kheh-rem] *under the ban, who may become doomed* [khaw-ram] *to destruction among men, shall be redeemed, but shall surely be put to death. And all the tithe of the land, whether of the seed of the land or of the fruit of the tree, is the Lord's. It is holy to the Lord.*

Studying this Hebrew word in Joshua opens our understanding to see the impact our tradition is having on the financial condition of the Body of Christ.

We find the word **kheh-rem** in Joshua 7:1:

But the children of Israel committed a trespass regarding the accursed [kheh-rem] *things, Achan the son of Carmi, the son of Zabdi, the son of Zerah, of the tribe of Judah took of the accursed* [kheh-rem] *things; so the anger of the Lord burned against the children of Israel.*

Achan took for himself what had been dedicated to God!

Joshua was fresh from a great victory at Jericho. He sent spies to Ai. The spies returned, saying, "Do not send everyone there. It is a small place. It is a waste for all the children of Israel to go up. Just send a few people up there and we will take it." Joshua sent three thousand men. They should have taken it, but they could not. They were beaten, and they did not know why.

Joshua fell on his face, crying, "God, why did You ever bring us over the Jordan?" As if to say, "God, it is your fault." God said, "Why are you crying and blubbering before Me, Joshua? Get up. There is a reason: The covenant has been transgressed." It is not working. Joshua 7:11–12 says:

Israel has sinned, and they have also transgressed My covenant which I commanded them. For they have even taken some of the accursed [kheh-rem] *things, and have both stolen and deceived; and they have also put it among their own stuff. Therefore the children of Israel* **could not stand** *before their enemies, but turned their backs before their enemies, because they have become doomed to destruction.*

Tithing Today

What does this account have to do with tithing today? God gave the tithe to the Levites. The five New Testament ministries of Ephesians 4 are among those who obviously qualify as modern-day Levites. They are apostles, prophets, evangelists, pastors, teachers.

When any one of these five claims for himself the whole tithe, he is spiritually doing exactly what Achan did physically—with the same impact on God's army. God said, "You are doomed to destruction. You cannot stand before your enemies." Studying this, I suddenly saw the full magnitude of what our enemy had accomplished through tradition.

In the majority of our churches every Sunday we say or imply, "It is time to bring the tithes and offerings into the storehouse." Many a message has been preached on the fact the storehouse is the local church, but we neglected the full truth. Nowhere in Scripture did God ever say He gave the tithe to the local synagogue. He said He gave it to the Levites. When any one of the New Testament Levitical ministries individually claims all the tithe without having a commitment to all five ministries functional and operational, he is doing to his people exactly what Achan did to Israel.

How many times has the local church been portrayed as the full storehouse, when it was at best only a partial one? When one man thinks he can do it all without any consideration for the remainder of the Levitical ministry, impurity reigns. God never intended that one gifting should bring a congregation of people to maturity. That concept is found nowhere in the New Testament. In fact, what is set before us as normal church structure is exactly the opposite. It takes input from all five gifts to bring anybody into the full measure of the stature of Jesus Christ.

The Theological Dictionary of the New Testament,[4] or *TDNT,* generally considered a definitive work in New Testament lexicography, says concerning the Greek word **ep-is-kop-os**:

> There is no reference to monarchical episcopate. [That means one-man traditional pastoral rule.] On the contrary, the evidence of the New Testament is clearly to the effect that originally several **episcopi** took charge of the communities in brotherly comity.

TDNT also indicates that in the early church, the only time pastors were in the pulpit was when the apostle, prophet, and teacher were out of town. After discussing the characteristics of the **ep-is-kop-os**, which is the Greek word usually translated "bishop," he says:

> There is a parallel passage in Titus 1:5–9. Titus had the task of appointing elders in the cities of Crete as Paul had done in Asia Minor according to Acts 14:23. This was the way to ensure the continued life of the churches once the missionaries had gone.
>
> The qualifications of presbyters here are like those of

---

4. *Theological Dictionary of the New Testament, Vol. II,* pp. 617, Edited by Gerhard Kittel, Translator and Editor Geoffrey W. Bromiley, D. LITT., D.D., Wm. B. Eerdmans Publishing Company, Grand Rapids, MI.

the bishops [**ep-is-kop-os**] in 1 Timothy 3:2 ff. In fact, there is an alternation of terms in Titus 1:7, where we suddenly have **epis-kop-os** instead of **presbuteros**. This is another proof that the two terms originally referred to the same thing, namely, the guidance and representation of the congregation and the work of preaching and conducting worship when there was no apostle, prophet or teacher present.

The picture presented is quite different from what we have inherited by tradition. By any one of the five ministry gifts claiming the tithe based on Malachi 3 ("Bring all the tithes into the storehouse. . ."), and disregarding biblical purpose for the tithe, which was for all Levites, we have corrupted the covenant and defiled the altar.

Twelve Corrupting Influences

By misusing Malachi 3:10, we have opened the door to twelve corrupting influences currently plaguing believers!

The twelve fruits of teaching the tithe as a formula are:

1. People become equated with money. Thus, the more people you get, the larger your budget.
2. Success in ministry is judged by numbers in the congregation, or on your mailing list, rather than fulfillment of the divine call.
3. Church growth becomes paramount and pressure to diminish the message to draw people seduces many leaders.
4. Competition for the saints among leadership grows because more people translate into more money.
5. Envy and jealousy rise among leadership over the size of their ministries.

6. Rich businessmen are recruited for special board positions, violating James 2 and the true purpose of deacons.
7. There is a growing pressure to refuse to preach anything controversial or offensive because it might dry up our funding.
8. Ministries are tempted to use Madison Avenue marketing techniques to woo people and build the mailing list, rather than praying for old-fashioned revival.
9. The saints are hindered in developing a confidence in hearing the Lord's voice through giving because they only relate to Him by formula.
10. Believers are strengthened in an unscriptural attitude of "works righteousness" by fulfilling a formula rather than learning to relate personally.
11. Many people are progressively overcome by discouragement because the promise of blessing and open windows never comes in the measure promised.
12. Fiercely sectarian doctrine arises, erecting barriers which keep the saints in "our" camp (the motivation is often financial), causing divisions and barriers hindering the unity of the faith which God has ordained.

Spiritual Politicians

Only the Lord knows how many organizations have been infiltrated by spiritual politicians who long to climb the ladder of success in position, power, influence, and prosperity, thereby defiling the altar rather than embracing the biblical motivation of service. The fruit of our inherited tradition is, in many places, apparent: Division, disharmony, disunity, and strife prevail.

In spite of our current state, I believe God has ordained the church to be the center of spiritual activity in these end-times. It is the place where spiritual "spot-remover" is applied, wrinkles are ironed out, and blemishes excised. I believe the church has been ordained of God to become the center of all activity where the supervision, training, and release of an end-time army brings in the greatest harvest the earth has ever produced.

During the decade of the '70s, there was a move of the Holy Spirit which seemed to be centered not in the churches, but in convention centers instead. The pastors of that era made the convention center ministries successful, because they would not allow emerging leaders in their pulpits.

Each of the five-fold ministries has a distinct and unique shepherding function, according to Acts 20 and 1 Peter 5, yet what distinguishes the shepherd from the shepherding function of the other four is the heart which he or she has for the people.

The Hireling Mentality

The difference between a true shepherd and a hireling is not difficult to spot (Mark 6:30–42). *The hireling is generally afraid to have other ministries of equal status around which he cannot control.* He wants everybody to know he is the undisputed, number one leader. Everybody else submits to him. He is everyone else's covering. Who is his covering? He submits to no man except to the Lord.

The hireling is generally afraid to have other ministries around because they are a threat to his position. He jealously guards position above everything else. The true shepherd, on the other hand, looks to his flock. He wants to make sure each of them is fed, and he realizes he usually has only one of the five ingredients necessary to bring them to a place of maturity and satisfaction in the Lord. The true shepherd actually encourages other ministries come in and bring his people the balanced diet they so desperately need!

In Mark 6:30–42 the Twelve were tired. They wanted to rest. They had not even had time to eat. Jesus demonstrates the heart of the true shepherd. He made them stay until the people's needs were met, recognizing one man could not serve by himself.

I believe the days of the one-man show are over. In days gone by, many congregations only had one man because that is all they could support. But as God restores ministry to the biblical pattern, He will raise up individuals who can and will gladly, willingly, go into churches, not requiring anything financially, even as Paul did, because they know God is involved in their ministry and will meet the need.

The true heart of the traveling ministry does not require a specified amount that unfairly burdens the local congregation. Neither do they leave unpaid bills behind when they leave town. The pure heart of a traveling ministry is to build up the local body and to deposit in the people the life that God has first put in them, believing and expecting that one place's abundance will take care of another place's lack. (For a more complete understanding of each gift and multiple-gifting, see the CD series "After God's Own Heart.")

The Five-Fold Ministry

Saints need the full input
To mature and to grow,
That no leader alone
Can impart or bestow.

Pure gifts given wisely
Provide just distribution,
Covering needed bases
For our wise God's solution.

CHAPTER 5

MANIPULATION, A MAJOR ROOT OF IMPURITY

If tradition is the number one source of impurity at the altar, it is only ahead of manipulation by a hair. Manipulation, like tradition, can be a part of your life as standard operating procedure and you do not even realize it!

In December 1984, the Lord spoke these words to me: "No longer sell your books and tapes, but make them available on a 'Pray and Obey' basis." January 1985 launched a learning adventure that lasted twenty-one years. After twenty-one years, God said, "You've learned what I wanted you to learn." "Pray and Obey" became a plumbline experience generating confrontation with the spirit of mammon.

Prior to "Pray and Obey," my experience had conditioned me

to believe that between fifteen and thirty percent of the monthly budget for traveling ministries came directly from the tape and book table. At that particular time, my ministry desperately needed a new car, walk-around microphone, and a variety of additional equipment totaling several thousand dollars. The money was just not available for any of it.

Nevertheless, I made the commitment to no longer sell books and tapes for one year. Looking up to heaven, with finger pointed at God, I said, "Lord, I am going to do this for one year, and if You do not honor it, that's all!"

So my initial commitment to "Pray and Obey" was for the year 1985. The second week of January, I was doing a seminar in a church in San Diego that had about five hundred people. The first night I explained the "Pray and Obey" concept, saying we no longer sold books and tapes. I walked back to the tape tables after the service, and we were swamped with what appeared to be two-legged vacuum cleaners snorkeling everything in sight!

I went back to the motel room that night and totaled up the cost to put everything on the table that had walked out the door. The total was $999.64 in actual cost or $2500 at retail value. In the "Pray and Obey" basket that night was $58.64. I looked up to heaven, pointed my finger at the Lord, and said, "This was *Your* idea, and it is not working!" Every week for the next three months, as I would get the ministry's weekly financial summary from my secretary, I was in utter amazement. It was as if God opened the windows of heaven for a season, and after three months of abundance, I was believing God again!

God's Way Works

The Lord honored that commitment. We were not only able to buy a car for our ministry, but one of equal value for a missionary, plus all the other equipment we needed. The Lord proved to me that He would supply the need of the ministry if I would but obey!

The thing that changed my life was what God said to me the night I returned from the first "Pray and Obey" meeting with only $58.64. I told the Lord, "This was Your idea, not mine, and it is not working." God's response to my prayer assault was 2 Chronicles 16:9. It was a verse I was familiar with in part. The part I recognized was:

> *For the eyes of the Lord run to and fro throughout the whole earth, looking for those whose heart is perfect toward Him, that He may show Himself strong in their behalf.*

I said, "Lord, what does it mean to have a perfect heart?" He said, "Go back to the beginning." The account deals with King Asa. To go back to the beginning, you have to return to 2 Chronicles, chapters 14–16. These chapters portray the life of Asa and what happened to him as a result of his choices.

Asa was a reformer with a very good heart and cleansed the land. Asa started out his ministry walking hand in hand with the Lord. He ". . . removed the altars of the foreign gods in the high places, broke down the sacred pillars, and cut down the wooden images. He commanded Judah to seek the Lord God of their fathers and observe the law and the commandments" (2 Chronicles 14:3–4).

Asa was unafraid to go to war. The Ethiopians came out against him with a million men and three hundred chariots, but because Asa readily acknowledged his utter dependence on God and was willing to go to war, God came through in his behalf. Asa was victorious over the Ethiopians, even though he was outnumbered two to one. Then came a warning:

> *The Lord is with you while you are with Him. If you seek*

Him, He will be found by you; but if you forsake Him, He will forsake you.

—2 Chronicles 15:2

There had been a famine of the teaching of God's Word in the land, and the prophecy came forth that restoration was the intent and plan for that season. Asa responded. Everyone followed his leadership and entered into a covenant to seek the Lord God with all their heart and with all their soul. The result was that God gave them twenty years of peace and blessing.

After these two decades of peace and prosperity, the enemy once again attacked Judah. Long periods of prosperity often results in spiritual passivity. The enemy cut off all of Asa's trade. Rather than going out to war, as he had done earlier, wholly trusting in God, Asa took the silver and gold from the treasuries of the house of the Lord and used them for another purpose!

He hired Ben-Hadad, king of Syria, who had always been an enemy of Judah, to go attack Baasha, king of Israel. This was common practice in the world of that day and it worked. King Asa got what he wanted, but he did not do it God's way. The Lord sent Hanani the prophet to rebuke Asa. His words are recorded in the second part of verse 9, which I had somehow missed: ". . . In this you have done foolishly; therefore from now on you shall have wars."

What Asa did was use *manipulation* to get what he wanted. Interestingly enough, it worked. But the price he paid to get what he wanted man's way was tremendous. Asa forfeited victories that God would have given him, and from that point on he would have wars because he was not willing to do what needed to be done God's way.

Spiritual law dictates whenever a ministry begins to use manipulation rather than trusting God financially, it will work for a season. The fruit of manipulation in the long term is continual financial wars. *Manipulation destroys our ability to walk with God.* Verses 12 and 13 of chapter 16 say:

> *And in the thirty-ninth year of his reign, Asa became diseased in his feet, and his malady was very severe; yet in his disease he did not seek the Lord, but the physicians. So Asa rested with his fathers; he died in the forty-first year of his reign.*

Asa abandoned his place of trust in the Lord, leaving only the physicians. There is nothing wrong with going to doctors. That is not what this scripture is teaching.

The Spirit of Manipulation

The latter end of Asa's life teaches us that the spirit of manipulation can gain such a foothold we no longer have a foundation on which to approach God in faith. It seems so easy to get what we want through manipulation—we lose our ability to trust God for it.

It is especially a warning to those of us who live in the last days when the spirit of manipulation will, in fact, become a very important part of the counterfeit trinity deceptively duplicating the move of the Holy Spirit. Examples of financial manipulation are more and more obvious, following the natural progression until destruction falls. One fundraiser I saw recently quoted scriptures out of the book of Acts:

> *And God wrought special miracles by the hands of Paul: So that from his body were brought unto the sick handkerchiefs or aprons, and the diseases departed from them, and the evil spirits went out of them.*

When you get a full-page color ad in the mail saying, "God told me to loan you a piece of my handkerchief," with an urgent return envelope, you should be suspicious. Examples of what can be done with the special handkerchief were given. You could lay it on a person for their healing, lay it on your old car for another one, lay it on your wallet for money to meet a budget or pay bills, lay it on your house for another one, and as you follow the steps that carefully tell you what to do, of course the last one says, "Return the handkerchief or prayer request and include the best gift you can come up with."

There is a major difference between what happened in Acts 19 and what is advertised in some cases today. The difference is Paul never sent his handkerchief with a return envelope telling people to immediately send back their best love gift. Paul's motivation was pure. I am not so sure about some of those I see today.

If you lay that fund-raising handkerchief on yourself, you are likely to get a double dose of the spirit that's driving the sender instead of Bible promises. It is very possible something can be transferred that you really do not want.

Classes in Fund-raising

Manipulation is being developed to a fine art. You can take classes in fund-raising and learn how to write appeal letters, or easier yet, buy a package of "proven performers" guaranteed to extract every available penny from every widow on your mailing list. Learning manipulation from the masters is a one-way ticket to a very shortened life in the Ananias and Sapphira tradition.

One of the quickest ways to defile an altar is to bring in professional fundraisers, who are generally paid a percentage of what they raise, which makes it quite obvious what their motivation is in everything they do. Any project that requires a professional fundraiser to bring it to pass, was probably not originated by God to start with. There is a world of difference between a professional fundraiser, who gets a percentage of what he collects, and a life coach who has been through the process and gives his time and energy to help entrepreneurs enter their giving ministry.

Like anything else Satan offers, once we start using manipulation, more is required each time to produce the same results. The pathway to addiction is the same for ministry business practices as it is for drugs, food or alcohol. The whole church can agree deliverance is needed for drug addicts, but the same deliverance is needed for some of our ministry business conduct because its roots are in the same demonic realm.

Mailing lists are bought and sold frequently in Christian circles today. That in itself is a violation of integrity. If you have ever received mail you did not request, your name and address was probably sold for a fee. We need a Holy Spirit vaccination against the disastrous deadly disease of manipulation. How can the church rescue the nation until God rescues the church?

We have a mailing list for a daily Bible study entitled the "Word At Work." We refuse to put people on it unsolicited. When one person requests we send it to a friend, we enclose a note saying, "We are sending you this material compliments of *your friend.* If you would like to continue receiving it, please return the enclosed card." Their name only goes on the list if they choose to continue receiving it. This is simple, basic, foundational ministerial integrity.

We have an obligation to teach believers how to discern the true from the false. If we are in a meeting and the big push for money comes forth—do we really think it is a manifestation of the Holy Spirit? We usually hear, "The Lord has impressed me that ten people are going to give $1,000, or twenty-five people will give $500" or, depending on the size of the meeting, "One hundred people will give $100, or five hundred will give $50."

When to Walk Out

If God really said that, what is the need for people to publicly stand and acknowledge the call which clearly violates Jesus' admonition to give in secret? This kind of fund-raising bears the marks of flesh, not spirit. If you are in a meeting and hear the words, "I am not going to preach unless we get $50,000," or whatever amount, do yourself a favor—get up and walk out. What God wants to do, He can pay for without man's help!

Even the Christian publishing world seems inundated with profiteers. When a new author first has a best-selling work, the publisher usually comes back immediately and pressures him for a second book. The publisher's motivation for a second work is usually financial. That defiles the work before it is ever written. Anyone who preaches or publishes what God gives for inordinate profit deserves to have some of the proceeds spent paying the personal expenses of an early departure. On two occasions in Jesus' earthly ministry, He "cleaned house" in the Temple. As we look at our church world today, it is obvious we are due for another one.

I do not believe there is anything wrong with selling books, CDs or DVDs. What defiles an altar is the *motivation* for advertising, production, and distribution. When we see a man in the pulpit taking an inordinate amount of time advertising his books and tapes, he usually is being pressured to meet his budget and without knowing it, has brought impurity to his altar.

When I told the Lord "Pray and Obey" was His idea and it was not working, He gave me 2 Chronicles 16:9 and said, "I finally got you in a place where I can bless you." I did not understand that. I had to pray and seek God for the interpretation.

Prior to January 1985, when I would go into churches where I knew my budget would probably not be met, sometimes I would take a few minutes to talk about books and tapes, because then people will go back to the tables and ask for them.

When I did this occasionally, I did not even realize what I was doing. You can do things in ministry because of pressure that your mind will justify.

What God was saying to me was, "Now that I have purified your altar by removing manipulation, I can begin to bless it." I believe the right attitude appears in the life of the Apostle Paul:

> *Did I commit sin in abasing myself that you might be exalted, because I preached the gospel of God to you **free of charge**? I robbed other churches, taking wages from them to minister to you. And when I was present with you, and in need, I was a burden to no one, for what was lacking to me the brethren who came from Macedonia supplied. And in everything **I kept myself from being burdensome** to you, and so I will keep myself. As the truth of Christ is in me, no one shall stop me this boasting in the regions of Achaia. Why? Because I do not love you? God knows!*
>
> —2 Corinthians 11:7–11

Motives for Publishing

Paul kept himself from being a burden to the churches. Today we make ourselves a burden. Paul was emphatic on one point: "There is one thing I live by. I preach the Gospel of Christ to you *free of charge*." I believe a principle that separates ministries is, "To what degree are we committed to this truth?"

How many Christian books would be written if they had to be made available without the promise of profit? There is nothing wrong with profit. Capitalism beats all comers. Motivation for the minister is paramount. "Would I publish if I never made anything?" is a monetary heart test. Ask it. That in itself would put the brakes on all projects being published for the wrong motivation. The issue is not the price on the product. If we can answer this question in the affirmative, "Would I offer this if I could not expect any profit from it?" then we publish.

Every man or woman called to full-time ministry must come to grips with 2 Corinthians 2:17 (NIV):

> *Unlike so many, we do not peddle the word for profit. On the contrary, in Christ we speak before God with sincerity,* **like men sent from God.**

The Greek word translated "peddle," is **kap-ale-yoo-o**, which has the following meanings, according to *The Hebrew-Greek Key Study Bible*:[5] "To treat as if for personal profit, profiteer, to adulterate the wine; to make a gain of anything. A huckster or petty retail trader. Adulterating not simply for the sake of it, but making an unworthy personal gain thereby. Profiteering from God's Word, preaching for money or professing faith for personal gain."

The Amplified Bible says:

> *For we are not, like so many (as hucksters, tavern keepers, making a trade of) peddling God's Word—short measuring and adulterating the divine message. . . .*

How would you define "short-measuring" the message? Refusing to address potentially offensive themes would qualify as short-measuring. How would Paul assess "seeker-sensitive" Christianity? When we have to spend twenty percent of our time advertising, promoting, and selling DVDs, books, or CDs just to stay on television or radio, God possibly did not call us to go on the air to start with. What God tells a man to do, He pays

---

5. *The Hebrew Greek Key Study Bible*, Lexical Aids to the New Testament, King James Version, Compiler and Editor Spiros Zodhiates, Baker Book House, Grand Rapids, MI 49506. Copyright 1984, p. 1700.

for without manipulation. How will we ever qualify for the next mighty move of the Spirit using such worldly tactics?

Peter demonstrates the mindset we need to have in Acts 3:6 when he says:

> *Silver and gold I do not have, but what **I do have** I give you: In the name of Jesus Christ of Nazareth, rise up and walk.*

In Acts 5, all who came for healing received. Do we *have* what Peter had? If not, why not?

Why could God trust Peter with that kind of authority but not trust our generation? The reason should be obvious. If there ever was a man who could easily profit from an anointing, it was Peter. People were healed when his shadow passed over them. Acts 5:16 records that every person who came was delivered and healed. Peter refused to advertise, sell or promote in order to personally profit from his anointing. His personal integrity opened the door to divine authority. Peter's attitude toward peddling is clearly revealed in his dealings with a new convert named Simon.

Before conversion, Simon was a magician making money through the magical arts. A common practice was to buy secrets from the great masters of the day, recouping your money from the people of your own city. Simon had apparently been successful because many called him "**. . . the great power of God**" (Acts 8:10).

The *Weymouth*[6] translation has excellent footnotes for the key words in Acts 8:18–23:

> *When, however, Simon saw that it was through the laying on of the Apostles' hands that the Spirit was bestowed, he*

---

6. Richard Frances Weymouth, *The New Testament in Modern Speech*, (London. James Clarke and Co., 3rd edition. Copyright 1911), p. 334.

offered them money. "Give me too," he said, "that power, so every one on whom I place my hands will receive the Holy Spirit." "Perish your money and yourself," replied Peter, "because you have imagined that you can obtain God's free gift with money! "No part or lot have you in this matter, for your heart is not right in God's sight. "Repent, therefore, of this wickedness of yours, and pray to the Lord, in the hope that the purpose which in your heart may perhaps be forgiven you. "For I perceive that you have fallen into the bitterest bondage of unrighteousness."

Peter was shocked and appalled that anyone would desire God's power for personal gain. Weymouth's footnote on the word "purpose" in verse 22 says, "The purpose was no doubt that of making money out of the spiritual gift."

The most sobering thing of all in this passage is how Peter viewed the spiritual condition of a man who would profiteer from God's giftings. Peter told Simon to repent, "in the hope that" he could be forgiven. *Weymouth's* footnote on the Greek says, "Lit. 'if (or, whether) therefore.' The exact sense seems to be, 'Find out by prayer *whether*, the offense being so *rank* and therefore the possibility of pardon so *doubtful*, the sin can nevertheless be forgiven.'"

Peter gave a powerful glimpse into God's heart concerning selling the gospel. The offense is so rank as to make forgiveness doubtful. By "selling the gospel" I mean the heart attitude *not* the price on the material. Could the Holy Spirit have been any clearer? Are we going to be ministers "sent from God," or powerless petty peddlers?

"Pray and Obey" has been a wonderful experience and we continue to honor it by offering the same teaching in Bible study format as is available in CD or book form, which can be purchased in our online store. The real issue is right motivation of the heart. If God is not in it, we had better not publish it. Paul made the gospel available to people freely believing God would pay for what He ordained. Can we make the personal commitment Peter and Paul made? Can we rise to that same level of faith?

Paul continues with this theme in 2 Corinthians 11:12–13:

But what I do, I will also continue to do, that I may cut off the opportunity from those who desire an opportunity to be regarded just as we are in the things of which they boast. For such are false apostles, deceitful workers, transforming themselves into the apostles of Christ.

True Apostles and Prophets

Pastors with pure hearts do not have to be afraid of the *true* emerging apostolic and prophetic ministries. This passage lays down a guideline to judge between the true and the false.

If someone comes saying, "I am an apostle," and demands you hand over authority in your church to him, or says he is a prophet and demands that you listen and act on his prophetic word without exhibiting the *service motivation*, he is generally a nut, flake, and allaround fruitcake!

The true emerging apostolic and prophetic ministries show the attitude of a servant. Some apostolic ministries are recruiting churches, asking them to give ten percent monthly of what comes in to their local churches according to Numbers 18 as God directed the Levites to support Aaron.

In the first place, Aaron is not, in most respects, a type of five-fold ministry. Aaron was a high priest for the people. There is only one High Priest in Christianity; His Name is Jesus. When Hebrews 7 says, ". . . his priesthood is not after the order of Aaron," it refers to the fact that Aaron died and his ministry ended. But Jesus is alive and His ministry never ends. Many of the things assigned Aaron were direct types of what Jesus would do for us. The five-fold ministry could never do what Jesus did.

To recruit churches at five or ten percent a month violates the very apostolic principle laid down by the Apostle Paul. He said in 2 Corinthians 11:12–13:

> *"I will continue to do what I do that I may cut off the opportunity from those who desire an opportunity to be regarded as true apostles."*

Paul said the difference between the true and false is obvious. The true do not require a set amount of money, demand quality amenities, and have to promote, advertise or market their works. The true can preach and publish without requirements, because they know God is involved in what they are doing. The false, on the other hand, which do not have the right motivation, have no guarantee of God's backing; therefore, they have to advertise, promote, require and demand.

The issue has never been the price on the material but the manipulation for mammon in the heart of the marketer. Not everyone who recruits churches at five or ten percent per month is a counterfeit. The real issue is motivation of the heart. If the motivation for ministry is financial, impurity reigns!

Paul's Pure Standard

The Apostle Paul set a pure standard. This principle in Paul's life is further borne out by looking in the Book of Philippians. The Apostle Paul visited Philippi during his second missionary journey and founded the church. He came back during his third missionary journey, and finally wrote the letter while he was in prison in Rome. At this point in time, Paul had three full missionary journeys behind him; he had established many churches, but what did he require of those churches he established?

Did he require ten percent of everything that came in every month? Did he require they put the building in his name? What did Paul require of the churches he himself founded? Philippians 4:15, written with just a few years remaining in his life, makes a strong statement for the way Paul conducted his relationship with the local church:

Now you Philippians know also that in the beginning of the gospel, when I departed from Macedonia, no church shared with me concerning giving and receiving but you only.

Paul had established other churches, but he did not require any support from them. He truly lived the principle he taught in 2 Corinthians 11. It is amazing to look at organizations that violate this principle today. Many denominations require a percentage, or at least the building or property in their name.

Practices such as this should flash at us like a blinking neon sign revealing true motivations of the hearts of men. When will we see the full covenant promises of God in manifestation? When once again our altars are pure and we can bring an offering to the Lord in righteousness.

Traveling ministries that make decisions about where to go based strictly on financial potential are in great danger of totally missing God. When the majority of pastors, who for years have faithfully served small congregations pay a price, how in good conscience can those of us who travel refuse to help based solely on their inability to pay? Are we serving God or man?

Any minister who recruits people for his "board," worship team, or any other position based on the wealth of the individual, will disqualify himself for participation in the next great move of the Holy Spirit. We need to ask ourselves about the real heart motivation for the things we do. What is our motivation for full-page ads in leading Christian publications? I was a Marketing major in college. Motivation of the heart is the issue, *not* the full-page ad. We cannot be promoters and qualify for the power at the same time.

To live the way Paul lived, we have to *know* God is involved in what we are doing. Today, in contrast, we can print our material in color, package, promote, and profit from it, and God help the people who buy it. To operate the way many of our churches and ministries operate today, God does not even have to be involved. *Which standard will we choose?*

As five-fold ministry gifts given to the Body of Christ, our assignment is to build Jesus into people, not build great ministries for ourselves. I believe God will no longer build great churches or ministries, but instead, He will build the Body of Christ. *Which standard will we support?*

Do you "peddle" for profit
As some tend to do?
Is it your desire
To bring gain back to you?

Corrupt profiteering
Comes in small degrees,
It will never, NO never
A HOLY GOD please

CHAPTER 6

THE OFFERING

In Malachi 3, God said, "You have robbed Me in tithes and offerings," making it quite clear the covenant includes both.

The purpose of the tithe is clearly stated, but what is the purpose of offerings? The first offering ever taken in Scripture was received in Exodus 25:1–2,8–9:

> *Then the Lord spoke to Moses, saying: "Speak to the children of Israel, that they bring Me an offering. From everyone who gives it willingly with his heart you shall take My offering. . . . And let them make Me a sanctuary, that I may dwell among them. According to all that I show you, that is, the pattern of the tabernacle and the pattern of all its furnishings, just so you shall make it."*

The offering was to build the tabernacle. One general rule consistently emerges: *offerings* in Scripture support *buildings*, while *tithes* support *people*. What usually happens on Sunday morning in a traditional church when a visiting ministry is present? The standard practice in many churches is to receive tithes and offerings for the local assembly first and then, after the guest has ministered, receive a love offering.

Depending on the inclination of the pastor, sometimes there is a five-minute exhortation about the necessity of the tithe given to the church. If all the tithers in Christendom had the testimony, "The windows of heaven are open," we would know we are operating correctly. However, when the majority of believers agree God's promises for tithing have not come, something is definitely wrong. Have our traditions made the Word of God of none effect? Does prevailing tradition have us using tithe and offering totally backwards? Is the tithe only Old Testament?

If Exodus 25 is not just a one-time event, and God expected people to continually use the offering for the building, we would certainly expect to see in Scripture other references to offerings used for buildings.

Solomon's Temple, after many years, fell into disrepair. The king in power at the time was named Jehoash. According to 2 Chronicles and the corresponding passage in 2 Kings, Jehoash, also called Joash, gave the following admonition:

> *And Jehoash said to the priests, "All the money of the dedicated gifts that are brought into the house of the Lord—each man's census money, each man's assessment money—and all the money that a man purposes in his heart to bring into the house of the Lord, let the priests take it themselves, each from his constituency; and let them repair the damages of the temple, wherever any dilapidation is found."*

Second Kings 12:4–5 becomes quite interesting when interpreted in the light of the corresponding passage in 2 Chronicles 24. There can be no doubt that these are offerings taken according to the commandment of Moses who initiated offerings for the Temple.

God is consistent. In His plan, the Temple or meeting place was built and maintained by offerings, while the Levites were supported through tithes. It is so complete and consistent in Scripture as to bring us to a place of conviction as to how we use tithe and offering today.

Three specific offerings are referred to: 1) census, 2) assessment, and 3) free will. In 2 Chronicles 24:5–6, the leaders were convinced God had ordained offerings to be taken, not tithes, for the preservation and continual upkeep of the building.

> *Then he gathered the priests and the Levites, and said to them, "Go out to the cities of Judah, and gather from all Israel money to repair the house of your God from year to year, and see that you do it quickly." However the Levites did not do it quickly. So the king called Jehoiada the chief priest, and said to him, "Why have you not required the Levites to bring in from Judah and from Jerusalem the collection, **according to the commandment of Moses** the servant of the Lord and of the congregation of Israel, for the tabernacle of witness?"*

God's Plan for Giving

This passage refers us back to Exodus 25, where the very first offering was taken. Using offerings for the building was God's plan then and seems to be now. It has always been God's plan. We have been taught offerings are for other ministries which come in as special guest speakers or for those outside the local church. What does this produce?

The fruit of this perversion is two-fold. First, it contributes to the testimony of the believers who have done their best to obey what leadership has taught by tithing faithfully, yet they have not seen the promise which was preached to them. Second, we see good men with excellent ministries pastoring when they could be much more effective in their true calling, but the local church has become the only place they can preach the tithe and pay the bills.

Competition between pastors and leaders of churches, which God never intended, has grown to an all-time high. Jesus clearly said, "A house divided against itself cannot stand," yet the competition from financial pressure is evident in practically every city in North America.

We will never have unity and harmony in leadership without a return to the biblical standard. The saints have to be released and taught to obey the leadership of the Holy Spirit, not a man's formula in giving. When a house of prayer is transformed into a den of thieves, Jesus will soon appear with broom in hand!

This heading appears in Deuteronomy 12 of *The Open Bible Study Edition*: "The Law of the Central Sanctuary." Today we do not have one central sanctuary nationally like Israel had, but the demand for purity is the same!

> *These are the statutes and judgments which you shall be careful to observe in the land which the Lord God of your fathers is giving you to possess, all the days that you live on the earth. You shall utterly destroy all the places where the nations which you shall dispossess served their gods, on the high mountains and on the hills and under every green tree. And you shall destroy their altars, break their sacred pillars, and burn their wooden images with fire. . . .*
> —Deuteronomy 12:1-3

Why did God say the impure altars had to be destroyed? *Whenever an individual participates at an impure altar, he is taking into his life the seed of the motivations of those who are operating that altar.* That seed will eventually be reproduced in him unless God intervenes. Impure altars defile the land by defiling the people. The motivation behind the activity makes it pure or impure. You can have two men trying to raise money for the same thing, yet one can be pure and the other impure. The difference is in the motivation of the heart.

Professional *fundraisers* brought into our churches generally bring manipulation and every unclean thing with them, profiting off the people of God by getting a percentage of the money they raise.

Any activity which requires the professional fundraiser in order to bring it to pass in the Kingdom has all the earmarks of being a man-made plan with the Holy Spirit nowhere involved. Every dollar weaseled out of believers by manipulation of any form is absolutely worthless as far as the covenant is concerned, and God is not obligated one whit to return it in any measure. In fact, what we often are participating in is not a covenant blessing, but can be a covenant judgment. Thank God, the Lord Jesus Christ is seated at the right hand of the Father extending grace to those of us who have been ignorant and out of alignment scripturally. This is the promise that covers us when we are unaware of the con job being perpetrated on us by the unscrupulous. God in His love can, through blood-bought grace, bless us for our giving anyway.

A great assault is prophesied for the church in the last days on the financial strongholds of the enemy. To be victorious in this season, we must be walking in God's covenant, standing firmly on His Word. We will never see these "wealth transfer" prophecies fulfilled if we remain ignorant and out of the way. No one possessed by a spirit of mammon can execute God's judgment on that spirit. Moses was not ready to execute judgment on the firstborn of Egypt when his own sons were unmarked by the covenant. God met Moses to kill him forcing the issue of compliance. Zipporah got the message and relented. Once Moses' family was obedient, God was ready to covenantally move on the enemy.

Recognize Manipulation

Several years ago, the Lord promised the day would come when the least discerning saint would be able to recognize when manipulation is present. Deuteronomy 12:5 states:

> *But you shall seek the place where the Lord your God* **chooses***, out of all your tribes, to put His name for His habitation: and there you shall go.*

The Hebrew root of the word for "habitation" is used for the abiding or settling of the glory cloud, signifying a time to stop and rest. Once again, God is going to reveal His glory and presence upon churches and ministries that are committed to pleasing Him. The glory cloud was a visible manifestation for all to see, recognizable by believers and unbelievers alike.

We have been conditioned to give by formula when there is apparent need. This is how ministries which are impure stay alive. *We have not taught the believers to get the voice of God and seek His face for direction on what to give where.* Instead of teaching God's people that their giving comes out of their relationship with the Lord, we have taught them to give by rote, rule, formula, and decree.

Tradition says ten percent belongs to the local church, and listen to God on your offerings, when the **truth** is you have to listen to God on everything. You have to listen to God about the amount of your offering and the distribution of your tithe. You have to listen to God about *everything*. It is only when we act on the voice of the Lord that we have the foundation to call forth covenant promises. Deuteronomy 12:13–14:

> *Take heed to yourself that you do not offer your burnt offerings in every place that you see; but in the place which the* **Lord chooses**. . . .

Whose choice is it? It is God's choice. Look at verse 19: "Take heed to yourself that you do not forsake the Levite as long as you live in your land."

The very institution God ordained both to teach His people and to provide for the Levites has victimized them. Our current church tradition is the lingering fruit of the fulfillment of Acts 20:29–31:

> *For I know this, that after my departure savage wolves will come in among you, not sparing the flock. Also from among yourselves men will rise up, speaking perverse things, to draw away the disciples after themselves. Therefore watch, and remember that for three years I did not cease to warn everyone night and day with tears.*

Can we recognize wolves? Many leaders have characterized lone individuals crying in the wilderness as wolves, but that defies all we know about a wolf pack. Wolves do not function alone. They join packs in a highly defined positional order. Wolf packs are dominated by alpha males who alone breed the females. Any other male attempting to breed is killed or isolated into compliance. When wolves meet, they raise hackles around the neck indicating position.

Recognizing wolves is easy. Look for the organization who wants you to join and consistently pay for the privilege (see "Beware of Spiritual Wolves" by Dr. Roger Sapp, AllNationsMinistries.

org). Attend a meeting and watch the hackles rise with the question, "How many attend your church?" I can imagine Peter walking into some of our "so-called" apostolic networks and reaching for the Ananias and Sapphira anointing. If the apostle Paul walked in to some of the meetings I have attended, he would have blinded the leaders in an "Acts 13 outburst of denouncing a false prophet with signs following." Lord, deliver us from wolves!

In many places, we have reduced the tithe to a formula, taken it for ourselves in the local assembly, and forsaken other Levitical ministries, bringing impurity to our altars and making the Word of God of none effect. Deuteronomy 26 reveals covenant relationship to us through the tithe. There are some who believe tithing is Old Testament and therefore is not applicable to those of us who live in New Testament times. This conclusion is often based on the assumption the tithe is a product of the Law, but Jesus said He came to fulfill the Law, not do away with it. God intended the covenant of the tithe to be a blessing, not a burden. While some ministers manipulatively mention Malachi, we cannot abandon biblical covenant because of those who pervert the Word for personal purposes.

In order to understand God's covenant, we must trace the tithe from its inception which came more than four hundred years before the Law was ever instituted. The tithe was never instituted by the Law. The Law gives insight into God's purpose and plan for the tithe. The Law itself does not apply concerning all of its different rules about the tithe today, but it does show us God's covenant purposes and plans. We would do well to remember the old evangelical saying, "The New Testament is in the Old Testament concealed; the Old Testament is in the New Testament revealed."

The Tithe

Studying Old Testament laws as they relate to the tithe helps us draw parallels in our understanding of *why* God instituted the tithe, and why Hebrews 7 says Jesus still receives tithes today. The New Testament witnesses to the current reality of tithing as the foundation of God's covenant for blessing and provision for man.

In Deuteronomy 26:12, God held the individual, not the synagogue, responsible for distribution. Instead of teaching people to pray about distribution, we have institutionalized the tithe and made offerings an after-thought. God always intended the giving of tithes and offerings to come out of our **relationship** with Him. This means we have to pray, receive direction, and be willing to act on what God speaks and leads us to do by His Spirit.

> *When you have finished laying aside all the tithe of your increase in the third year, which is the year of tithing, and have given it to the Levite, the stranger, the fatherless, and the widow, so that they may eat within your gates and be filled, then you shall say before the Lord your God: "I have removed the holy tithe from my house, and also have given them to the Levite, the stranger, the fatherless, and the widow, according to all Your commandments which You have commanded me; I have not transgressed Your commandments, nor have I forgotten them. "I have not eaten any of it when in mourning, nor have I removed any of it for any unclean use, nor given any of it for the dead. I have obeyed the voice of the Lord my God, and have done according to all that You have commanded me."*

God expected His people to be able to look up to heaven and command the fulfillment of a promise. Verse 15 is explicit. The people were supposed to say to the Lord:

> *"Look down from Your holy habitation, from heaven, and*

bless Your people Israel and the land which You have given us, just as You swore to our fathers, 'a land flowing with milk and honey.'"

Today, that "land" is our nation, state, business, company family and job.

Commanding the Blessing

There is no way you and I can command the blessing God promised if we do not have a platform of obedience. In order to command the blessing of verse 15, the Jews had to obey the admonition of verse 14.

When we can clearly say to God, "I have obeyed your voice. sent exactly what you spoke to me exactly where you said it should go," *then* we can call for the multiplication and the blessing God intended as a result of our being obedient in both tithe and offering.

By reducing tithe to a formula, we have separated God's people from any need to pray and hear the voice of the Lord. This removes the platform for realizing the promises of verses 17 and 18. Deuteronomy 26, verses 17 and 18 (KJV), give us a foundation to stand before God and command a budget to be met:

> *Thou hast avouched the Lord this day to be thy God, and to walk in His ways, and to keep His statutes, and His commandments, and His judgments, and to hearken unto His voice: And the Lord hath avouched thee this day to be His peculiar people, as He hath promised thee, and that thou shouldest keep all His commandments.*

The first time I read "avouched" in the King James Version, it flashed like a neon sign and I thought, "What in the world is an 'avouch'?" It must be important, because God promises if we can do it, "He will set us high above all nations which He has made, in praise, in name and in honour . . ." (verse 19).

This promise is in the context of obeying the voice of God in distributing the tithe. You are going to be the head and not the tail, above and not beneath, if you can "avouch." God promises that He will set us not just above, but *"high above."*

Is the church high above? Or are the unbelievers high above?

> . . . *and that He will set you high above all nations which He has made, in praise, in name, and in honour, and that you may be a holy people to the Lord your God, just as He has spoken.*

Being able to "avouch" is obviously the key to seeing God's promises in manifestation. But what does "avouch" mean? It is the Hebrew word **amar.** According to *Gesenius' Hebrew Chaldee Lexicon to the Old Testament,* it is used in this passage as a **hiphel** verb. A **hiphel** verb is a causative verb. Causative means when we do what we are supposed to do, we cause happenings to take place as a result of our action activating the covenant.

Our activity sets in motion a chain of events which will cause a promise to come to pass, and all of heaven waits on us to initiate it by obeying God's Word. This scripture says when we can pray and say, "God, I have obeyed Your voice," we cause God to do something.

Gesenius says, "Thou hast this day made Jehovah say, or promise, etc.; verse 18, 'And Jehovah hath made thee promise, i.e. you have mutually promised, and accepted, and ratified the conditions *of each other.*'"[7] Can we set forth conditions? The Lord led

---

7. *Gesenius' Hebrew Chaldee Lexicon to the Old Testament* (Baker Book House, Grand Rapids, MI. Translated by Samuel Prideaux Tregelles LL.D. Copyright 1979. First printed 1857 Samuel Bagster and Sons, p. 61.

me to this passage in 1980. At that time, I had been in the radio ministry almost a year, and felt led to go on a number of additional stations. This suddenly brought a dramatic increase in our monthly budget. The monthly radio bill was now equal to the budget for the rest of the ministry, which effectively doubled our monthly bills.

I was feeling the pressure. I prayed, "God where am I going to get the money to pay for the stations I believe You led me to go on?" My problem was, I did not have the faith to operate at the new level of financial necessity. The Lord led me to Deuteronomy 26, and the word "avouch" leaped off the page like a blinking, neon sign. When I discovered the causative covenantal meaning of "avouch," I knew I would never have to worry about a budget again, as long as I could look up to heaven and say, "Father, I have obeyed your voice!" Because it is a causative verb, it means when I take the time to pray, listen to Father's voice, and act on it, I cause Him to listen to my voice and respond to my need.

Gesenius' statement is amazing in its ramifications for every believer. He said, "You have mutually promised, and accepted and ratified the *conditions of each other.*" Because I did what He told me to do, He will do what I ask Him to do. *Because I obeyed and gave where God told me to give, He will work and bring to pass what I tell Him I need.* This truth only works when I am obedient to the best of my ability, doing the whole counsel of God's will. God's covenant is awesome. This kind of relationship is far from formula!

Free From Financial Pressures

This truth relieved me from all financial pressure. I knew regardless of how many stations God told me to go on, whether radio, TV, or whatever the project, I would never again have to worry about a budget as long as I obeyed. If the budget is not being met, either severe warfare has come, or I have to seek God about obedience.

When God has called you to head a ministry, and He brings more and more people on board, suddenly you are obligated for thousands of dollars in salaries, rental contracts, and so forth, with many people dependent on you. How do you walk in perfect peace in the middle of the financial pressure without yielding to manipulation, which is the temptation and tendency of so many?

Many of our Christian media programs are full of manipulation. The commercialization of the gospel is at an all-time high. Everywhere we turn, we are being offered or sold something which is *guaranteed* to bring us a new level of blessing, peace, and joy. Merchandising God's Word, self-promotion, and advertising His gifts with a mixed seed motive is an abomination!

When the foundation of an altar is impure, the truths taught there avail nothing, and the Body of Christ continues to struggle from day to day. We have inherited a system which is often corrupt by tradition, but we live in a timeframe when God has promised to restore the foundations. He has promised prophetically a transfer of wealth to the church for the purpose of a great end-time harvest; not for the purpose of individual blessing, and not for the purpose of making a name for ourselves, bathing in the glitz and the glory of personal pursuit.

Many pastors rightly criticize traveling ministries for selling and manipulating in fund-raising, but they seldom realize that the way they teach the tithe falls into the same category. The whole system has to be turned upside down in order for us to walk before God right side up.

The traditional way we have taught the tithe has removed the biblical foundation for the individual believers being able to stand before God and decree covenant blessing. Our current tradition allows charlatans and manipulators to preach the tithe for their own selfish ends, bringing disrepute to God's path for provision. God called those of us in leadership to be men and women who help open the windows of heaven, but in many cases, through tradition, we have closed them. *God will open the windows of heaven when we purify altars and walk in the way of His Word!*

*When the altar
Is pure,
Your foundation's
Secure.*

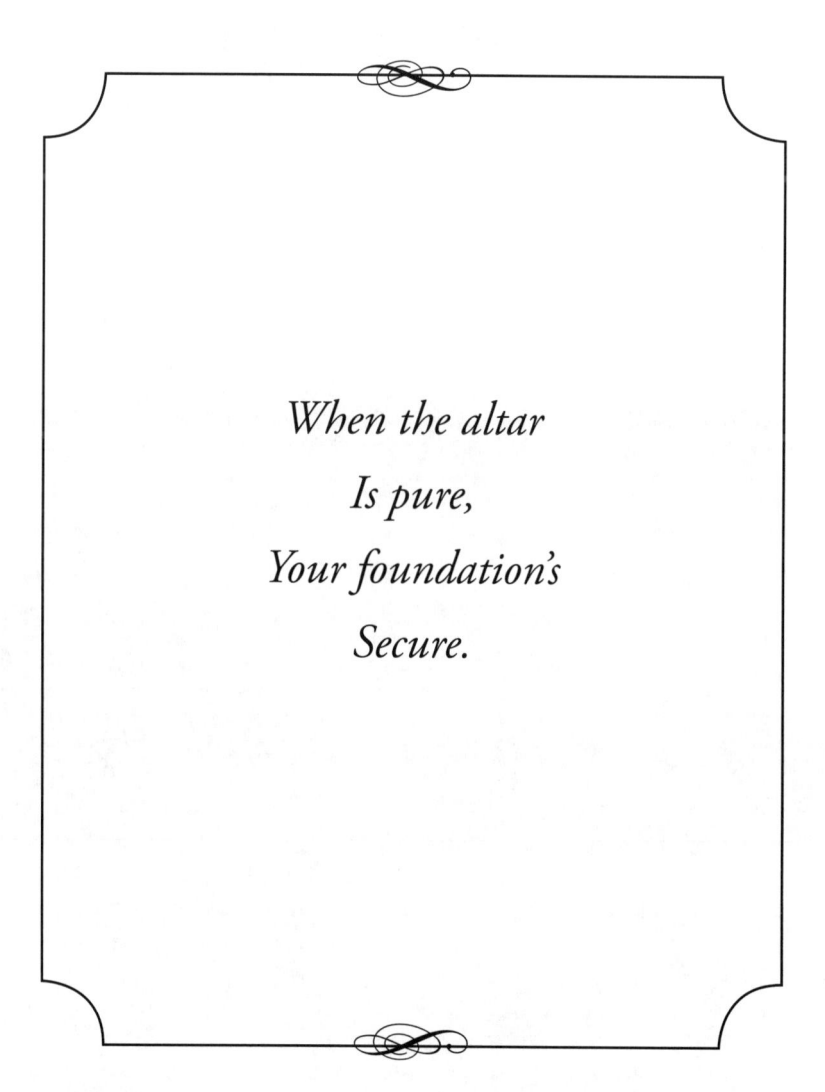

CHAPTER 7

THE SPIRIT OF AMMON

Nehemiah was called to bring restoration. He began his ministry during the reign of Artaxerxes I of Persia, 464–423 B.C. Queen Esther was Artaxerxes' stepmother and was possibly instrumental in Nehemiah's appointment as the king's cupbearer.

From the time of Israel's emergence as a nation, the Ammonites were their most persistent and consistent enemy. They helped hire Balaam. Sihon, the king of Ammon, had a portion of territory given to Israel and had to be subdued. They sought every opportunity to humiliate Israel and retake the territory. Ammon oppressed Israel during the reign of the Judges, nearly conquered Jabesh-gilead in Saul's reign, treated David's ambassadors disgracefully and invaded Judah under Jehoshaphat. They united with Hazel in Syria's oppression and took all the territory they could possess. The people of Ammon were consistently ruthless in opposition to God's covenant people. Their persistent hatred of Israel began to reflect the nature and characteristics of a strong demonic spirit.

Nehemiah's assignment to rebuild the temple is a perfect example of spiritual warfare against a supernaturally energized enemy.

Nehemiah left Persia in the twentieth year of Artaxerxes' reign and returned in the thirty-second year, leaving again for Jerusalem after a few days. His heart was definitely in rebuilding Jerusalem. His assignment was to help the restoration by rebuilding the walls and strengthening the people of the Lord. Nehemiah faced tremendous opposition, which came in stages. Nehemiah 2:9–11 outlines both his purpose and the source of opposition:

> *Then I went to the governors in the region beyond the River, and gave them the king's letters. Now the king had sent captains of the army and horsemen with me. When Sanballat the Horonite and Tobiah the Ammonite official heard of it, they were deeply disturbed that a man had come to seek the well-being of the children of Israel. So I came to Jerusalem and was there three days.*

Nehemiah first encountered the spirit of Ammon upon his return to Jerusalem. *The spirit of Ammon is absolutely opposed to any restoration and blessing God would like to bring to His people.*

Nehemiah laid out his purpose and gathered the Jews, exhorting them to rise up and build.

> *But when Sanballat the Horonite, Tobiah the Ammonite official, and Geshem the Arab heard of it, they laughed us to scorn and despised us, and said, "What is this thing that you are doing? Will you rebel against the king?" So I answered them, and said to them, "The God of heaven Himself will prosper us; therefore we His servants will arise and build, but you have no heritage or right or memorial in Jerusalem."*
> —Nehemiah 2:19–20

The foundation of the war had already been laid. Nehemiah

declared his God-given purpose. The spirit of Ammon began to rise up in alliance with others to thwart God's plan. Through ridicule, mockery, persecution and using political government, they attempted to stop God's purpose. The church's enemies today use government to thwart God's purpose, steal religious freedom and ban biblical opposition. In 1960, as a supporter of John F. Kennedy, I got in a fist fight with my nearest neighbor who supported Richard Nixon. If I vote for the party of my youth today, I vote for people who have vowed to put me in jail for preaching Leviticus 20 or Romans 1. One political party is determined to criminalize Scripture as "hate speech" by imposing jail time on ministers for stating what God thinks about homosexuality. Once again, Nehemiah had to say, "The God of heaven Himself will prosper us; we His servants will arise and build, but you have no heritage or right or memorial in Jerusalem." That was a very important statement. Nehemiah 4:1–3 states:

> *But it so happened, when Sanballat heard that we were rebuilding the wall, that he was furious and very indignant, and mocked the Jews. And he spoke before his brethren and the army of Samaria, and said, "What are these feeble Jews doing? Will they fortify themselves? Will they offer sacrifices? Will they complete it in a day? Will they revive the stones from the heaps of rubbish—stones that are burned?" Now Tobiah the Ammonite was beside him, and he said, "Whatever they build, if even a fox goes up on it, he will break down their stone wall."*

When demons move people to oppose our God-ordained purpose, God expects us through covenant to invoke Spiritual Judicial Authority. God-assigned purposes often grind to a halt under the weight of demonic opposition. At this point, we must arise and call for covenantal intervention. Let the Judge of all the earth arise for the church, just as He has in days of old. Davidic psalms are recorded for examples of how to pray, what to ask and what to expect. Nehemiah's wall could not have been built without Spiritual Judicial Authority. Hear the heart cry of the builders and take note. When Democrats or Republicans are so possessed by a spirit of Antichrist that they vote to advance a perverse agenda that can be used to jail pastors and priests, then the time to invoke Divine Justice has come. Let today's Herods who desire to silence the church be silenced as Herod was. Verses 4–5 say:

> *Hear, O our God, for we are despised; turn their reproach on their own heads, and give them as plunder to a land of captivity! Do not cover their iniquity, and do not let their sin be blotted out from before You; for they have provoked You to anger before the builders.*

Why have we not used David's example and prayed his prayers? (For an understanding of this realm, see *The Sure Mercies of David*.)

> *So we built the wall, and the entire wall was joined together up to half its height, for the people had a mind to work.*
> —Nehemiah 4:6

Nehemiah finished the first stage of what he was called to do in Jerusalem, and for a season he had to return to his position at court to report again to the king. During the few years Nehemiah spent with the king, Tobiah, who was an Ammonite, began to find other ways he could hinder the restoration process in Jerusalem.

A man named Eliashib became high priest in Jerusalem. Eliashib, along with the other priests, helped rebuild the Sheep Gate, according to Nehemiah 3:1. As high priest, he could assign chambers in the Temple to whatever purpose he pleased. Tobiah married into Eliashib's family and secured a position God never intended him to have.

> *On that day they read from the Book of Moses in the hearing of the people, and in it was found written that no Ammonite or Moabite should ever come into the congregation of God, because they had not met the children of Israel with bread and water, but hired Balaam against them to curse them. However, our God turned the curse into a blessing. So it was, when they had heard the Law, that they separated all the mixed multitude from Israel. Now before this, Eliashib the priest, having authority over the storerooms of the house of our God, was allied with Tobiah. And he had prepared for him a large room, where previously they had stored the grain offerings, the frankincense, the articles, the tithes of grain, the new wine and oil, which were commanded to be given to the Levites and singers and gatekeepers, and the offerings of the priests. But during all this I was not in Jerusalem, for in the thirty-second year of Artaxerxes king of Babylon I had returned to the king. Then after certain days I obtained leave from the king, and I came to Jerusalem and discovered the evil that Eliashib had done for Tobiah, in preparing a room for him in the courts of the house of God. And it **grieved me bitterly**; therefore I threw all the household goods of Tobiah out of the room.*
>
> —Nehemiah 13:1–8

The spirit of Ammon had set itself up in the storerooms and completely controlled them. Balaam is a good example of one who yields to the spirit of Ammon. For honor and money, he sold out and tried to curse the people whom God wanted to bless. Because God would not let him curse Israel, he sold Moab and Ammon a plan which would defile the covenant people!

The Moabites and Ammonites in return got temporary victory over Israel, because Israel could no longer stand in their covenant, once impurity had a foothold. The covenant would no longer work on their behalf; therefore, they could easily be conquered.

What was the fruit of Tobiah's new residence? It is clearly given in verses 9 and 10:

> *Then I commanded them to cleanse the rooms; and I brought back into them the articles of the house of God, with the grain offering and the frankincense. I also realized that the portions for the Levites* **had not been given them; for each of the Levites and the singers who did the work had gone back to his field.**

When Ministry Is Thwarted

When the spirit of Ammon gets involved in the storehouse, it will drive all the Levites out to their fields. No longer was the full flow of ministry available for God's house. When Tobiah, who represents the spirit of Ammon, controlled the storehouse, the Levites could no longer work together as God intended.

When Tobiah set up his home in the storehouse intended for the Levites, *the purpose and plan of God was immediately thwarted.* The Levites had to "work their own fields" or, in our vernacular, find a secular job, no longer devoting themselves to prayer and the ministry of the Word.

This was apparently the condition of the Temple under the scribes and Pharisees. In Acts, chapters 4 and 5, two different hearts are contrasted: one pure and one impure. Barnabas is contrasted with Ananias and Sapphira as an example of what God was doing in the church.

> *Now the multitude of those who believed were of one heart and one soul; neither did anyone say that any of the things he possessed was* **his own**, *but they had all things in common.*
> —Acts 4:32

When Tobiah set up his house in the storerooms, everything that came in was *his own* or under his control to do with as he wanted. But when the true heart of God is in manifestation, there is care one for the other, and recognizing the need of others supersedes personal ambitions. Acts 4:33–37 records:

> *And with great power the apostles gave witness to the resurrection of the Lord Jesus. And great grace was upon them all. Nor was there anyone among them who lacked; for all who were possessors of lands or houses sold them, and brought the proceeds of the things that were sold, and laid them at the apostles' feet; and they distributed to each as anyone had need. And Joses, who was also named Barnabas by the apostles (which is translated Son of Encouragement), a Levite of the country of Cyprus, having land, sold it, and brought the money and laid it at the apostles' feet.*

Just as the Levites fled to their own land and were forced to make a living outside of God's intended purpose when Tobiah set up shop in the storehouse, so today the same fruit is seen in the New Testament. The spirit of Ammon is still alive and well!

The Levites were to wholly give themselves to God's Word, teaching and training the people, that there be no plague among the Israelites when they came into the Temple. But when the spirit of Ammon took over, the Levites were forced out. They had to find their own jobs or till land God had intended only for grazing.

When Joshua conquered the land of Israel, the Levites were given cities and land for cattle, but were told not to till the field as the other Israelites did. The Levites' "produce of the field" was to come through the tithes of the people. Joshua 21:1–3 records:

> *Now the heads of the fathers of the Levites came near to Eleazar the priest, to Joshua the son of Nun, and the heads*

of the fathers of the tribes of the children of Israel. And they spoke to them at Shiloh in the land of Canaan, saying, "The Lord commanded through Moses to give us cities to dwell in, with their common-lands for our livestock." So the children of Israel gave to the Levites from their inheritance, at the commandment of the Lord, these cities and their common-lands.

It would appear that Barnabas the Levite was forced to work a secular job because the system had degenerated to the place where it was much like what Nehemiah found upon his return to Jerusalem. Barnabas had to wait until God said, "Now is the time to quit your secular job, sell your land, plant the seed, and go into ministry. You have been called for years, but only now is the framework in place where you can be supported."

Another New Testament figure, Luke, was trained to be specific in his duties as a physician. It appears he was equally as precise in the words he chose as a writer. He used words like a mechanic uses tools.

Kho-ree-on is one of the two Greek words for "land" which generally indicates space, place, region, district, piece of land, a field, a city and its environs, i.e., the region around a city closely related economically and politically.

Ag-ros, on the other hand, according to *Bauers Lexicon*, is a plot of ground used mainly for agriculture, i.e. a farm.[8] *Weymouth*, in his translation of Acts 4:37, says, "a farm."[9] *Vines* denotes **ag-ros** as a field, especially a cultivated field; hence country in contrast to town.[10] Luke used **ag-ros**, not **kho-ree-on**, as one would expect if

---

8. Bauer, Walter, *A Greek-English Lexicon of the New Testament*, edited by Arndt & Gingrich, University of Chicago Press. Copyright 1957, p. 13.
9. Richard Frances Weymouth, *The New Testament in Modern Speech*, (London. James Clarke and Co., 3rd edition. Copyright 1911), p. 322.
10. W. E. Vine, *An Expository Dictionary of the New Tesatament*, Fleming H. Revell, 17th Impression. Copyright 1966, p. 92.

the land was being used in harmony with Levitical purpose.

The Greek word for "having" in verse 37 is *hoop-ar-kho*, "to begin below, to make a beginning to come forth," giving us the indication that the beginning of Barnabas' ministry took place when he sold and then planted the seed from the field. *Ow-tos* of *ow-tos ag-ros* means "self" as used in all persons, genders, and numbers to distinguish a person or thing from or contrasted with another or to give emphatic prominence. The Greek sentence structure makes prominent the fact that Barnabas sold **ag-ros**, not **kho-ree-on**. **Kho-ree-on** would tend much better to describe the kind of land Levites were to have according to God's plan, but the word used to describe what Barnabas had was **ag-ros**, indicating Barnabas was in the same position as the Levites Nehemiah found when he returned to Jerusalem. Such is the fruit in any generation when the spirit of Ammon sets up his house in the church.

Defiling the Altar

There is an entirely different spirit at work in the church which Jesus initiates. *The spirit of Ammon fully defiles an altar and turns it into a place of self-advancement, rule, and promotion.* Nehemiah had to kick Tobiah out and then cleanse what had been defiled. Nehemiah 13:11–13 states:

> *So I contended with the rulers, and said, "Why is the house of God forsaken?" And I gathered them together and set them in their place. Then all Judah brought the tithe of the grain and the new wine and the oil to the storehouse. And I appointed as treasurers over the storehouse Shelemiah the priest and Zadok the scribe, and of the Levites, Pedaiah; and next to them was Hanan the son of Zaccur, the son of Mattaniah; for they were considered **faithful**, and their **task** was to **distribute** to their brethren.*

Which spirit rules over the storehouse? Is there a dedication to distribute to the brethren and have the full flow of all five ministries functional and operational as soon as possible? Or is the commitment to build "me" a ministry? In Acts 4, when the money was laid at the apostles' feet, they did not use it solely for themselves. It was distributed to those who had need. Luke 22:24–27 says:

> *But there was also rivalry among them, as to which of them should be considered the **greatest**. And He said to them, "The kings of the Gentiles exercise lordship over them, and those who exercise authority over them are called 'benefactors.' "But not so among you; on the contrary, he who is greatest among you, let him be as the younger, and he who governs as he who serves. "For who is greater, he who sits at the table, or he who serves? Is it not he who sits at the table? Yet I am among you as the One who serves."*

We serve people when we provide all the input they need to mature, equip them to accurately discern true from false, and fulfill God's call on their life. God never intended one man to do that by himself. *I believe the next move of the Spirit will be centered in the local church, but the spirit of Ammon will have to be prayed out first.*

When we put money on an impure altar, God is not obligated one iota to return it. What is the motivation which governs the storehouse where you attend? Is it really a storehouse, or is it masquerading as one? Is it, in fact, a dwelling place for Tobiah?

There are many men God has called to walk in five-fold ministry positions who are working secular jobs because Tobiah is living in the storehouse. If Tobiah is alive and well in your church, go to God in prayer and demand the purifying of the altar, and somewhere, somehow God will intervene!

Is the spirit of Ammon
Active…up and running,
By the misuse of money
Through greed and great cunning?

When "Tobiah" is working
And settled to stay,
The storehouse is challenged
To function God's way.

May we worship at altars
God-pleasing and pure,
May honoring God here
Be the goal and the cure.

CHAPTER 8

THE ANOINTING TO SPOIL

Several years ago, the Lord posed these questions to me: "Son, how did I build My sanctuary? Where did My people get the money for the Tabernacle of Moses and for the Temple of Solomon? Did the money come from their jobs?"

I replied, "I do not know."

He said, "Well, find out."

That encounter initiated a search of Scripture which changed my understanding of God's financial plan. Exodus 12:35–36 says:

> Now the children of Israel had done according to the word of Moses, and they had asked from the Egyptians articles of silver, articles of gold, and clothing.

And the Lord had given the people favor in the sight of the Egyptians, so that they granted them what they requested.

The Hebrew word used here translated favor is **khone**, which is a derivative of **khow-nan**, carrying the image of the stronger and the weaker in negotiation. The Egyptians, strong in military might and wealth, were weak when God began to move in behalf of His people. The last part of verse 36 says, *"Thus they plundered the Egyptians."*

When the Israelites came out of Egypt, God put an anointing on them. "They borrowed from the Egyptians." Whoever translated the Hebrew as "borrowed" had a sense of humor. They certainly did "borrow," but with no intention of ever giving it back. *They spoiled Egypt!*

This was my introduction to an aspect of God's plan I had never seen or understood before. The Lord said, "What about the Temple of Solomon?" There apparently has never been anything on the face of the earth that even approaches the value of the Temple Solomon built.

The image of the weak underdogs made strong through God's anointing and consequently taking what God wanted them to have further develops, and perhaps crystallizes, in 1 Chronicles 22, beginning in the first verse:

> *Then David said, "This is the house of the Lord God, and this is the altar of burnt offering for Israel." So David commanded to gather the aliens who were in the land of Israel; and he appointed masons to cut hewn stones to build the house of God. And David prepared iron in abundance for the nails of the doors of the gates and for the joints, and bronze in abundance beyond measure, and cedar trees in abundance; for the Sidonians and those from Tyre brought much cedar wood to David. Now David said, "Solomon my son is young and inexperienced, and the house that is to be built for the Lord must be exceedingly magnificent, famous and glorious throughout all countries. I will now make preparation for it." So David made abundant preparations before his death.*

How much did David prepare? More importantly, how did he get it? Verses 13–14 tell us:

> *Then you will prosper, if you take care to fulfill the statutes and judgments with which the Lord charged Moses concerning Israel. Be strong and of good courage; do not fear nor be dismayed. Indeed I have taken much trouble to prepare for the house of the Lord one hundred thousand talents of gold and one million talents of silver, and bronze and iron beyond measure, for it is so abundant. I have prepared timber and stone also, and you may add to them.*

The weights and measures conversion tool of *Logos Bible Software*[11] sets one talent of gold at $8,640,000, therefore the Temple gold was worth $864 billion. The silver value is set at one-tenth of the gold, making one talent of silver worth $864,000. One million talents of silver would be in value exactly equal to the gold or $864 billion. How did they get so much money? According to 1 Chronicles 26:26–27:

> *This Shelomith and his brethren were over all the treasuries of the dedicated things which King David and the heads of fathers' houses, the captains over thousands and hundreds, and the captains of the army, had dedicated. Some of the **spoils** won in battles they dedicated to maintain the house of the Lord.*

Building With Satan's Money

God's warriors received from Him an anointing to spoil, and out of that spoil His house was built. This second Temple was built with the world's money. *God's buildings were built with Satan's money.*

---

11. *Logos Bible Software X,* Scholar's Library Gold, Logos Bible Software, 1313 Street, Bellingham, WA 98225-4307

Is the "Anointing to Spoil" really for today? Just because God released it initially for Israel while in Egypt and through David's army does not mean it is for the New Testament church. This was precisely my thinking when the Lord led me to Isaiah 53, the great prophetic glimpse of all Jesus bought and paid for in the atonement. Verses 10–12 state:

> *Yet it pleased the Lord to bruise Him; He has put Him to grief. When You make His soul an offering for sin, He shall see His seed, He shall prolong His days, And the pleasure of the Lord shall prosper in His hand. He shall see the travail of His soul, and be satisfied. By His knowledge My righteous Servant shall justify many, For He shall bear their iniquities. Therefore I will divide Him a portion with the great, And He shall **divide the spoil** with the strong, Because He poured out His soul unto death, And He was numbered with the transgressors, And He bore the sin of many, And made intercession for the transgressors.*

This passage says Jesus bought and paid for an "Anointing to Spoil" which He will parcel out in the last days. On this point, many scriptures agree, including the words of the Lord Himself. Matthew 12:28–29 say:

> *But if I cast out demons by the Spirit of God, surely the kingdom of God has come upon you. Or else how can one enter a strong man's house and **spoil his goods**, unless he first binds the strong man? And then he will spoil his house.*

The Greek word translated "spoil" in Matthew 12:28–29 is **dee-har-pad-zo**. It is the strengthened form of the root word **har-pad-zo** which, according to *Lexical Aids to the New Testament*,[12]

---
12. *The Hebrew-Greek Key Study Bible, Lexical Aids to the New Testament,* King

means "to strip, spoil or snatch, literally to seize upon with force," differing from **klep-to**, which means to steal secretly. It is an open act of violence in contrast to cunning, secret thieving.

Dee is an intensive, and is used to strengthen the force of the already strong word **har-pad-zo**. **Har-pad-zo**, without the strengthened addition of **dee**, appears in a very familiar passage, 1 Thessalonians 4:17:

> *And so shall we be caught up* [har-pad-zo] *together with the Lord and so shall we ever be with the Lord.*

Majoring in the Wrong Rapture

When we look at the force of the basic word used in 1 Thessalonians 4:17 for "rapture," versus the strengthened form used in Matthew 12:28–29, one truth quickly emerges: I believe many leaders over several decades have majored on the wrong rapture!

More authority and power will be released in the horizontal rapture than will be released in the vertical one. Many teachers have emphasized the Lord taking the church out, when we should have emphasized the church taking spoil away from the devil. The *vertical* rapture will take care of itself. The *horizontal* one has to be done in the open. A brute display of force, not one done in secret, is the one we need to major on for today's church.

Jesus will display more **doo-nam-is** power and **ex-oo-see-ah** authority through the church in the last days, destroying the works of the devil and bringing in an end-time harvest, than will be needed when He catches up the church to meet Him in the air. Jesus personally divides the "Anointing to Spoil" with the strong. The first and primary fulfillment is Psalm 2, while the secondary fulfillment is Isaiah chapters 60 and 61, both fitting together as pieces of the same puzzle. Psalm 2:7–9 says:

James Version, Spiros Zodhiates, Th.D., Compiler and Editor, Baker Book House, Grand Rapids, MI 49506. Copyright 1984, p. 1670.

I will declare the decree: The Lord has said to Me, "You are My Son, Today I have begotten You. "Ask of Me, and I will give You the nations for Your inheritance, And the ends of the earth for Your possession. You shall break them with a rod of iron; You shall dash them in pieces like a potter's vessel."

This aspect of the "Anointing to Spoil" deals with the harvest of souls which has to come from the nations. We should forget about the Lord coming any day to take us out until we fulfill His revealed purposes now. It is time to prepare for the greatest confrontation, persecution, and warfare the church has ever known as we put our shoulder to God's purpose of bringing in a harvest of lost souls. How can we expect God to take us out when the greatest harvest ever awaits?

Without the other aspect of the "Anointing to Spoil," it is difficult to harvest souls. I am speaking of the fulfillment of Isaiah 60 and 61 as it relates to the church.

Isaiah 60:1–5 says:

Arise, shine; For your light has come. And the glory of the Lord is risen upon you. For behold, the darkness shall cover the earth, And deep darkness the people; But the Lord will arise over you. And His glory will be seen upon you. The Gentiles shall come to your light, And kings to the brightness of your rising. Lift up your eyes all around, and see: They all gather together, they come to you; Your sons shall come from afar, and your daughters shall be nursed at your side. Then you shall see and become radiant, And your heart shall swell with joy; Because the abundance of the sea shall be turned to you, The wealth of the Gentiles shall come to you.

Isaiah 61:6–7 stresses God's commitment to fulfill His promises to the church:

But you shall be named the Priests of the Lord, Men shall call you the Servants of our God. You shall eat the riches of the Gentiles, And in their glory you shall boast. Instead of your shame you shall have double honor, And instead of confusion they shall rejoice in their portion. Therefore in their land they shall possess double; Everlasting joy shall be theirs.

Financing the Harvest

Prophetically, the church has to bring in a harvest. This requires the releasing of a unique anointing in the last days. The harvest has to be financed, which, in turn, requires the release of another anointing. "The Kingdom of God is upon us," means the rule, reign, and authority of Jesus Christ. We are commanded to occupy or, as *The New King James Bible* puts it, "do business" until the King comes. That business requires a progressive outpouring of the "Anointing to Spoil!"

I was on my way to conduct a Bible study meeting on a Tuesday night and suddenly the Spirit of God came upon me and I started to cry. I could hardly see the freeway. I was praying and weeping before God in a burst of intercession when suddenly out of my spirit came the interpretation: "God, if pastors will not support the five-fold ministry, give me the money and I will." That night in the meeting, a businessman walked up and put a check for $18,000 in my hand! I went out the next morning and took a check to a prophet of God. His wife had tears in her eyes and said, "This will be the first time since October (this occurred in March) of last year that we have been current in paying our bills."

And we wonder why the windows of heaven are not open to the Body of Christ. I thank God for revealing His heart to me through a visitation of the Holy Spirit. As a result, I began to make a commitment to use my faith for other ministries.

We do not want to be shepherds who care only about ourselves. A selfish financial attitude initiates a dangerous spiritual progression, according to Isaiah 56:10–11:

> *His watchmen are blind, They are all ignorant; They are all dumb dogs, They cannot bark; Sleeping, lying down, loving slumber. Yes, they are greedy dogs, Which never have enough. And they are shepherds who cannot understand; They all look to their own way, Every one for his own gain, From his own territory.*

We can safely say God will not release anything through altars dominated by such defiled hearts, which are continually looking for their own gain from their own quarter. We are entering a season where using our faith more for others than ourselves is required. God's heart is held in reserve for such yielded vessels!

I see in Scripture a harvest prophesied for the last days in which every nation will hear God's Word and respond. Where will the money come from to mature the fruit of this revival? The anointing will flow upon those chosen, and they will take their place like David, who prepared with five smooth stones to destroy the giant. Where do we presently stand in this progression?

Pure Altars Needed

Not only are the windows of heaven not open corporately, but the "Anointing to Spoil" is not flowing as it should individually in the Body of Christ. The "Anointing to Spoil" will be released through pure altars. *The flow depends on the heart of the one responsible for the ministry.* This anointing will take the world's money to finance God's purposes and plans, not man's.

The same God who swept physical dictators from power to open the borders of Eastern Europe will sweep away spiritual dictators so the five smooth stones, signifying the five-fold ministry, can prepare the local Body.

This anointing brings with it a weighty responsibility. According to 1 Samuel 30:21–24, some of David's army did not want to share with those who stayed with the supplies. Only when the heart of sharing is established in an individual, can he expect to receive God's anointing to move in the dimension of spoil.

Now David came to the two hundred men who had been so weary that they could not follow David, whom they also had made to stay at the Brook Besor. So they went out to meet David and to meet the people who were with him. And when David came near the people, he greeted them. Then all the wicked and worthless men of those who went with David answered and said, "Because they did not go with us, we will not give them any of the spoil that we have recovered, except for every man's wife and children, that they may lead them away and depart." But David said, "My brethren, you shall not do so with what the Lord has given us, who has preserved us and delivered into our hand the troop that came against us. "For who will heed you in this matter? But as his part is who goes down to the battle, so shall his part be who stays by the supplies; they shall share alike."

When God releases the "Anointing to Spoil," we have the responsibility to dispense it accordingly. If our hearts are not settled on this issue, we will never qualify for this anointing. The "Anointing to Spoil" was bought and paid for at the cross. Isaiah 53, which gives us great prophetic insight concerning what was accomplished there, states very clearly in verses 10 through 12:

Yet it pleased the Lord to bruise Him; He has put Him to grief. When You make His soul an offering for sin, He shall see His seed, He shall prolong His days, And the pleasure of the Lord shall prosper in His hand. He shall see the travail of His soul, and be satisfied. By His knowledge My righteous Servant shall justify many, For He shall bear their iniquities. Therefore I will divide Him a portion with the great, And He shall divide the spoil with the strong, Because He poured out His soul unto death. . . .

The Word is very clear in outlining the fact that, while He was on the cross, Jesus paid a price for this anointing to flow in the Body of Christ. He will see it come into manifestation in the last days, funding the greatest revival the earth has ever seen.

Pastoring Your Business

At one point, I was preparing for a marriage seminar in Washington, D.C. I went in the office on my day off to pray and ask the Lord about direction concerning what He wanted me to share during that marriage seminar. He would not speak one word to me about the marriage seminar, but began to talk instead about "Pastoring Your Business." I knew it was a message for the Sunday morning prior to my flying to Washington, D.C.

I saw men who were gifted and called of God to a ministry which was every bit as important as standing in the pulpit. Yet their ministry was not a pulpit ministry. Their ministry was in the business world, and the Lord made me to understand that His concept of administering both was the same. Businessmen were to begin to look at their businesses just as a pastor looks at his church. They were to pray for it, impart the vision to employees, receive the wisdom of God through intercession, and consequently would face the same kind of resistance and warfare.

That encounter with the Lord produced a two-CD series entitled, "Pastoring Your Business." It was one of about five events over a five-year period that God used to broaden my understanding, preparing me for a ministry to businessmen.

Three years later, the Lord impressed me to hold my first

Businessmen's Seminar. He instructed me to lay hands on people, planting and calling forth the "Anointing to Spoil." As I sought the Lord about the restoration of the "Anointing to Spoil," I began to sense it, too, would be restored in reverse order.

When it first appeared in Scripture, in Exodus 12, the whole body of believers participated. The second time we see it in Scripture, it is not the whole body, but only a selective group. It is seen upon David's army as led by his "Mighty Men."

Just as God has restored the five-fold ministry of Ephesians 4:11 in reverse order, it appears He plans the same pattern for the "Anointing to Spoil." The early church was birthed under the administration of apostles. They nourished and restored the prophetic—God had been silent four hundred years. They taught and trained teachers. They prepared and released pastors. They recognized and energized evangelists. What was first in the early church seems to be restored last now.

The "Anointing to Spoil" Jesus purchased in the atonement as outlined in Isaiah 53:12 has a very different application under the judicial auspices of each of the five governmental gifts. Each gift/office reflects a specific piece of Jesus' heart. An evangelist reveals God's heart for the lost. When this heart cries for the "Anointing to Spoil," the fruit should parallel a cascading stream of Billy Graham crusades. When a pastor cries for the "Anointing to Spoil," he wants God's anointing to destroy the problems of his people. A wave of deliverance and victory would result. When a teacher cries for the "Anointing to Spoil" revelation comes from heaven that transports the church into a new paradigm (see *The Sure Mercies of David*). When a prophet cries for the "Anointing to Spoil" he can find himself confronted with a conflict of governments as Elijah in 2 Kings 1:9–15:

> *Then the king sent to him a captain of fifty with his fifty*

men. So he went up to him; and there he was, sitting on the top of the hill. And he spoke to him: 'Man of God, the king has said, "Come down!"' So Elijah answered and said to the captain of fifty, 'If I am a man of God, then let fire come down from heaven and consume you and your fifty men.' And fire came down from heaven and consumed him and his fifty. Then he sent to him another captain of fifty with his fifty men. And he answered and said to him: 'Man of God, thus has the king said, "Come down quickly!"'; So Elijah answered and said to them, 'If I am a man of God, let fire come down from heaven and consume you and your fifty men.' And the fire of God came down from heaven and consumed him and his fifty. Again, he sent a third captain of fifty with his fifty men. And the third captain of fifty went up, and came and fell on his knees before Elijah, and pleaded with him, and said to him: 'Man of God, please let my life and the life of these fifty servants of yours be precious in your sight. Look, fire has come down from heaven and burned up the first two captains of fifties with their fifties. But let my life now be precious in your sight.' And the angel of the LORD said to Elijah, 'Go down with him; do not be afraid of him.' So he arose and went down with him to the king.

When the "Anointing to Spoil" manifested, the king's servants died; God backed the prophetic office so that the gift "spoiled" the enemy and won the conflict of governments. Jesus bought and paid for our access to this anointing through the atonement. Each office is responsible for developing faith to function in this realm as it relates to their specific piece of Jesus' heart for the Body. The full measure of God's government will be released to confront the demonized demigods in political government! When the real prophets rise, the fire will fall.

"The Anointing to Spoil"

A God-structured transfer
Is going to occur,
Through many anointed
Assigned and made pure.

Involving a plan that
The Lord's set in place,
With hearts free of greed
Greatly flowing in grace.

Funds repositioned
Our enemy we'll foil,
And the weapon of choice
The "Anointing to Spoil."

CHAPTER 9

PREPARING TO SPOIL

Pastoring Mighty Men

The Holy Spirit has seeded into the church a select group of mighty men just as He graced David with those who shared his heart for covenant victory. One unique characteristic of mighty men is a growing fearlessness in their forte. For those in business, the fearlessness would manifest in the "art of the deal." They repeatedly are willing to lay everything on the line for the next acquisition almost impervious to the potential for failure.

"Mighty men" often combine the gift of faith and boldness, making pastoring them nearly impossible. They pioneer like Abraham, often looking for a city whose builder and maker is God alone. The most challenging period of their life is the transition from conquistador to conservator and each one has to make it.

It is in this season that "mighty men" achieve their greatest potential for the Lord because they can become mentors for the next generation instead of simply collecting coupons for a leisurely life. When we fail to reproduce our heart, we forfeit a generation. The American church is losing the nation when Jesus promised if we would ask, He would give us our nation. The church today needs "mighty men" as never before as we resurrect the warrior's heart and impart to an emerging generation a spirit honed for decades in the crucible. God is about to pour forth the heart of "mighty men" as liquid gold upon a generation who does not know war!

A few years after the Lord gave me the concept of "Pastoring Your Business," He spoke to me on the first day of my vacation to study Isaiah 23–24 in *The Living Bible*.[13] In *The Living Bible*, Isaiah 23 deals with the restoration of businesses which recognize their purpose of supporting ministry.

I knew this would be a selective group that we would first see moving in the "Anointing to Spoil" financially. I never dreamed there was a manifestation to be possessed by ministers, based on their five-fold governmental office. Eventually, we will see measures of it restored in the Body of Christ.

I have received the testimonies of businessmen who have put these principles into practice and seen God greatly multiply their ministries. One man shared that his business had grown in two years from five employees to 135. He initiated prayer meetings and healing services for his employees, and said he spent a fair amount of his time just ministering to their needs. That is not for every company. The key is to be led by the Holy Spirit.

He looked at his business as a pastor looks at his flock, helping and caring for the people whom God sent to work there. He prayed for them, and was determined to serve them. God honored him to the extent that bankers saw the success he was enjoying and came to offer credit lines. The secular world views the boss as one who must be served, but the Bible teaches the attitude of a servant is what qualifies us to be the boss. Success can come much more quickly when we agree with God's principles.

---

13. *The Living Bible*, Tyndale House Publishers, Wheaton, IL 60187. Copyright 1984, pp. 467, 468.

There is much God wants to do in the last days, and many ministries have to be supported. We are coming into a season when God is releasing the "Anointing to Spoil," because Jesus paid for it in the atonement. Some will use it to take money from the world which is needed for training the next generation. Running a business is every bit as much a call of God as the call to stand behind the pulpit. Business requires an anointing, just like ministering to a congregation. It takes a heart to serve and a willingness to obey the leadership of the Holy Spirit. It also requires a unique preparation because dealing with mammon is like assaulting the foundation of Satan's throne. The "Anointing to Spoil" is a judgment. In order for us to execute it, the prince of this world can have nothing in us if we are to be successful.

Faithfulness Disregarded

The blind greed of some in corporate America has caused a curse to settle on their businesses that only restitution can remove. Firing people just prior to their qualification for vesting in pensions or dismissing other long-term corporate obligations just to save money recklessly disregards years of faithful service. Corporate raiders destroy years of hard work and goodwill with a ruthless motivation for profit, caring not about the lives they disrupt or careers they devastate. They need to be spoiled.

God wants to raise up a standard in stark contrast to many in the current business climate. The "Anointing to Spoil" will be given to those who recognize their biblical obligation to serve their employees and commit to act accordingly. When God finds such committed hearts, there will be a supernatural transfer of business from the greedy to the gracious. Where is our heart? It takes longer to prepare a man for success than anything else.

Jesus bought and paid for the anointing to possess a harvest from the nations and fulfill the promise of Psalm 2:8, "Ask of Me and I will give You the nations. . . ." The process of bringing a harvest nationally is one that requires a tremendous amount of funding. The Bible has a lot to say about God's intent.

The prophets proclaim a transfer of wealth in the last days that Satan has hoarded through deception. I believe the testimony of Isaiah, and other prophets, reveals God's plan to raise up an army of business people to bring a transfer of wealth into the Kingdom for this great end-time harvest. There is probably no assignment that carries a greater price than this because we know that money is the very foundation of Satan's throne. He uses the love of it just as God does the Holy Spirit in the life of a believer. Actually, manipulation and the spirit of mammon work together to counterfeit the work of the Holy Spirit gaining worship for Satan. When a believer conquers mammon, he is ready for a promotion into the anointing experienced by David's Mighty Men.

I believe that *Purifying the Altar* is a tool to aid leaders in releasing the "Anointing to Spoil" and activating God's army to fulfill their prophetic purpose. In this process, it is helpful to be able to look at people who have walked the preparational path and learn from their mistakes. God will often save us decades of preparational time if we can learn from the life of others. With that hope in mind, David Lu offers his testimony of God's preparational path for the "Anointing to Spoil."

David Lu's Testimony

When God prepares a vessel for the "Anointing to Spoil," crucifixion is the general path until the character of Christ is formed—and there is no escape. David Lu grew up in a small town in central Taiwan worshipping ancestors in local temples, as was the family custom.

David's first miracle came through a culture where marriages were arranged by parents. An attractive young lady named Grace from a Christian family accepted his proposal. Like Abraham, David had to leave his culture to really find God. During a war between China and Taiwan, Grace's older brother, who was in America at the time, came back to Taiwan to apply for emigration for her whole family to go to the United States. Because of the war, the U.S. government issued the visas much faster than usual. Within a few months, visas had been approved.

In June of 1978, David and Grace arrived on U.S. soil. Learning English was a major barrier but essential for God's path of blessing. Grace worked in a restaurant while David tried to find a good job. They wanted to quit and return to Taiwan many times, but persevered, obeying the leadership of the Spirit.

David's response to a Sunday sermon was a desperate prayer. "God, we came to the U.S.A. based on Your will. Please help me find a job that would make it so we can stay in the U.S.A. I am not asking to become rich. I am just asking to take care of my family. If this is not Your will for me, then I will return to Taiwan." Two weeks later a man invited David to his office for an interview, but he could not understand the directions. That evening, he had a friend counsel him on how to react in the interview. The friend said to be very confident and not humble like the old Chinese way. The next morning, David brought an abacus (an ancient counting tool) to the interview. He was applying for a bookkeeper job. When they saw him using the abacus they told him that no one uses an abacus in America. They then showed him their accounting books. He had never seen that type of bookkeeping before and had never used an adding machine in Taiwan.

At that point, David did not feel he could say, "I can't handle the bookkeeping job." At the end of the interview, he told the owner that accounting was universal. "We import accounting textbooks from the U.S.A. so we have the same accounting terminology. If you let me try for one week, I will know how to do your bookkeeping. I will work for you for one week for free, and then you can decide if you want to keep me or not." The owner was impressed with David's offer. He replied, "No one in the U.S. would work even for one hour for free." He got the job.

David worked for the company for eight years and was promoted to vice president of finance. The company grew from 1,000 to over 100,000 square feet of space in eight years. It grew in personnel from less than 10 to more than 100 employees. God knows how to multiply. (Initiating the Anointing to Spoil demands that pioneering participating parties gain a "vehicle" which God can bless. Either buying or starting your own business is helpful!)

David says of his transition: "In 1981, my brother started a PC manufacturing and exporting business in Taiwan and begged me to help him by opening a sales and distribution office in the U.S. as my own company. The business grew into a full-time job."

Into Temptation and My Downfall

The business grew very rapidly. At the time, our largest customer was PC Limited, which eventually became Dell Computer. In five years, our business grew to fifteen times its original size. In 1992, *INC 500* named DFI the ninth fastest-growing private company in the USA. Suddenly, we became very well known in the PC industry. In the meantime, we opened distribution centers in New Jersey, Florida and San Jose, bought a mail order company in Phoenix, and partnered with a company in Dallas. The group revenue grew up to $120 million a year. At that time, many companies in the PC industry were going public and making a fortune, so I started to dream about making a fortune, too. Our company had 140 employees; more than 30 of them were church family. On the outside I was very humble, but my inner man became very proud, and my heart started looking for financial gain more than anything else—just like Lot.

Because of God's blessing, all my business ventures were very successful, so I decided to pursue a public offering. A consulting firm suggested business revenue of at least $250 million per year to qualify. It was not easy to double the business in such a short time, so I figured the only way to reach that target revenue was to merge with another company.

On a trip to San Jose to collect the past due payment of "M" Company, I met with the owner's wife. She told me that because her husband was in the last stage of cancer, the company was being mismanaged and she needed help. She agreed to give up half of the company's interest to me. I assumed it was from God that I was looking for a company to merge with, and suddenly there was a company with revenue of about $120 million per year asking for help. I met with their banker and signed a personal guaranty for "M" company while providing product for the company to sell. I began to visit weekly to try to clean up their books and push sales. I gradually became attracted to Mrs. "H," who was an idol worshipper and believed in fortune telling, but I was not bothered by that and sinned against God. After three months of diligently trying to turn around "M" company, I found out it was impossible. Not only did I lose the money that I invested in that company, but I needed to deal with their bank about my personal guaranty. Pride goes before a fall!

Repentance and Restoration

. . . God opposes the proud but gives grace to the humble.

—James 4:6

. . . My son, do not make light of the Lord's discipline, and do not lose heart when he rebukes you, because the Lord disciplines those he loves, and he punishes everyone he accepts as a son.

—Hebrews 12:5

Purifying the Altar

Unless the Lord builds the house, its builders labor in vain. Unless the Lord watches over the city, the watchmen stand guard in vain.

—Psalm 127:1

During my trial, I learned a very good lesson called "humility" through repentance, forgiveness and restoration.

A prophetic minister encouraged me with a vision: He saw that I was climbing very high on a pole, and suddenly I fell down. He saw a group of chickens fighting for my food. He told me that God had some words for me: "Because you honor your parents, God will remember you. Because you have helped many people, God will remember you, and God will help you and pull you out of your trouble." What a word of comfort. It came at the time when I was in deep, deep trouble.

Within a month, I was able to shut down the Miami office, sell the Phoenix company and terminate the partnership with the Dallas company. My brother took over the New Jersey and the San Jose offices, and suddenly my burden was reduced by five-sixths. I then sold my 50,000-square-foot office building without putting up a "For Sale" sign. The buyer paid $200,000 more than my asking price. After I sold my office building, I got a call from a real estate broker that told me there was an industrial building looking for sublease at a very low price. It happened that the space just met our needs. So from selling the building to moving into the new space with all our equipment and furniture, it all took place within three months. It was absolutely amazing.

God Made a Way

Isaiah 43:19 says, "I am making a way in the desert, and streams in the wasteland." God did.

After I cleaned up all of my mess, I asked God if He wanted me to quit the business or not, because at that time, I had downsized the company from 140 employees to around 15. Sales revenue went down from $4 million per month to around $200,000 per month. We continued to suffer a loss every month. Again I prayed with some prophetic pastors, and they all gave me the same vision and message that God would give me a second chance, and my future business would be better than the previous, and God would return all the money that I had lost. I believed in faith even if the circumstances looked very bad. At that time, even big companies could not survive. So how could I do better than they could? But I did not try to explain or argue; I knew only time would prove God's Word.

Finally in November 2003, we received an order from a business that we had been working with for the previous two years. When we received the order, I just knew our company was about to be reborn.

In 2004 and 2005, God let me earn back all the money I had lost. Thank God that He is a living God, full of mercy and love. He will make miracles happen in our lives, even if sometimes we have sinned against Him. But if we truly repent, He will forgive all of our sins."

David Lu's testimony reminds me of the promise of Joel, chapter 2, verses 23–27, concerning the preparation and execution of the "Anointing to Spoil." This passage says:

> *Be glad then, you children of Zion, And rejoice in the LORD your God; For He has given you the former rain faithfully. And He will cause the rain to come down for you—The former rain, And the latter rain in the first month. The threshing floors shall be full of wheat, And the vats shall overflow with new wine and oil. So I will restore to you the years that the swarming locust has eaten, The crawling locust, The consuming locust, And the chewing locust, My great army which*

I sent among you. You shall eat in plenty and be satisfied. And praise the name of the LORD your God, Who has dealt wondrously with you; And My people shall never be put to shame. Then you shall know that I am in the midst of Israel, And that I am the LORD your God And there is no other. My people shall never be put to shame.

God promises that He will bring a double portion anointing in the last days and restore all that was lost during the years of preparation. In this passage, we see the God of the "suddenly" revealed in personal revelation as He promises to bring an end to devastating circumstances and restore the original vision. In Joel 2:26, he uses the Hebrew word **paw-law** talking about God dealing wondrously with us. **Paw-law** means to go beyond the bounds of human power or expectation. **Paw-law** is used in Genesis 18:14 when the angel says to Sarah, who was laughing at the thought of having a child at her age, "Is anything too **paw-law** for God?" Joel 2:27 goes on to say that once we experience God's "suddenly" in fulfillment, then we shall ". . . know . . . [**yaw-daw**]" which is the Hebrew word for the ultimate of intimacy in the physical union. There is a "knowing" of God that is reserved for those who through a long season of devastation "suddenly" find God fulfilling what He had promised years ago. This is the God that takes people off the dung hill and sets them among princes. Such is the consistent prophetic preparational process that seems to be part of executing what the prophets called, the "Anointing to Spoil." David Lu experienced this process. Let his testimony be an encouragement to any who will find the God of the "suddenly" in the days ahead as He restores them and brings the finances for a mighty end-time harvest. The God of the "suddenly" is visiting the church!

The devastation
Will not always be,
Trust God, seek to "know" Him
One day you will see.

That day you will see
And perfectly know,
Why circumstances
Just had to be so.

Beyond our own labors
Or human design,
He'll come in great glory
King Jesus Divine

The "suddenly" washes
The anguish away,
The King of Glory
He will have His way

CHAPTER 10

JUDGING RIGHTEOUS JUDGMENT

Judging righteously in judgment is one of the most difficult tasks facing believers in these times. There are always those who are quick to judge and blast everyone who does not measure up to the standard they feel appropriate. And yet, on the other hand, there are many who think it is absolutely too dangerous to make any judgments at all. This latter attitude is a by-product of taking Matthew 7:1–2 out of context:

> *Judge not, that you be not judged. For with what judgment you judge, you will be judged; and with the same measure you use, it will be measured back to you.*

On the surface, this passage seems to present an open and shut case, but on the other side of the proverbial coin is 1 Corinthians 5:11–13:

> *But now I have written to you not to keep company with anyone named a brother, who is a fornicator, or covetous, or an idolater, or a reviler, or a drunkard, or an extortioner—not even to eat with such a person. For what have I to do with judging those also who are outside? Do you not judge those who are inside? But those who are outside God judges. Therefore "put away from yourselves that wicked person."*

It is quite obvious from this passage that the Holy Spirit expects us to be a people who are equipped to judge righteously, yet the warning of Matthew 7 should ever be before us. To say we are to never judge within the Body, based on Matthew 7:1, is absolutely a perversion of Scripture. It is not true. We are forced to make judgments within the Body of Christ.

What, then, is Matthew 7 dealing with? It is dealing with the proper attitude that enables us to judge with righteous judgment. Matthew 7:3–5 says:

> *And why do you look at the speck in your brother's eye, but do not consider the plank in your own eye? Or how can you say to your brother, "Let me remove the speck out of your eye"; and look, a plank is in your own eye? Hypocrite. First remove the plank from your own eye, and then you will see clearly to remove the speck out of your brother's eye.*

The warning of Matthew 7 cannot be construed to say we never judge; rather, this is the criteria by which we approach making judgments within the Body.

Judging Ourselves

First, before we make declarations concerning the failure of others, we must seek the Lord to see if the presence of the same thing is in ourselves. To judge the local altar where we attend as impure, we must first ask God to show us the impurity in our own lives. Then and only then can we approach judgment with the motivation of restoration and not from a position of hypocrisy, which demands God's dealing with us.

"Judge not, that you be not judged" is not a prohibition against making judgments concerning leadership or anyone else in the Body, as has been so prevalently taught, but rather is a warning to us about *how* we go about making such judgments. Verse 4 says, ". . . how can you say to your brother, 'Let me remove the speck out of your eye'; and look, a plank is in your own eye?"

How easy it is to cause offenses when we make judgments because of a self-righteous attitude which exists due to our negligence in obeying this principle. To reach maximum effectiveness in bringing individuals to restoration through confrontation, we first must search our own hearts and let God show us the very same things in our lives that we have begun to see in the lives of others.

Then and only then can we approach people with compassion, because God has shown us where we have violated the same principle. To restore a brother and remove sin from his life, we first must seek God to remove the same sin from our own lives. Following these guidelines will help bring restoration rather than offense and destruction. God's purpose is to restore the Body, not destroy it.

If we would leave Matthew 7:1–12 in context, we would have no problem. In Matthew 6:1–4, Jesus said, "Give, but don't give like the hypocrites." In verses 5–15, He said, "Pray, but don't do it like the heathen." In verses 16–18, He said we should fast, but not like the hypocrites. Judging follows in the same context. We can judge, but if we judge as the hypocrites, God guarantees judgment in return.

Judgment is necessary, but it can only be done in the right spirit, when we judge ourselves first. God honors confronting errant behavior with compassion when the motivation is to restore!

We must remember that one violation of any principle outlined in this book does not provide grounds for labeling the offender false, counterfeit or having an impure altar.

Selling the Anointing

I will never forget the first time a nationally-known minister promised a believer his prophetic anointing for a $50,000 donation in exchange for his watch. The event was a fundraiser for a local church, so only God knows how much he pocketed, but when this becomes a pattern, major defilement spreads like spiritual cancer.

The question remaining is, what becomes of the life of the donor when he realizes he gave $50,000 but got a $50 watch and a promise of anointing? Has that poor fellow been set up for shipwreck? The judgment on the manipulator should be no less than what Ananias and Sapphira got!

When can you judge a person a false prophet? We must realize that good people sin. Just because a person sins does not mean he is false or counterfeit. When we see sin, we have a Christian obligation to confront, expecting repentance and restoration. If offering his watch for thousands and promising his anointing reoccurred over and over, then we see the behavior of a false prophet.

When a person refuses to accept our individual correction, we should take one other person with us who was involved, knows, or has seen the offense. When an individual refuses to accept the second witness and continues manipulating or offending, manifesting no evidence of repentance, then we can judge their work false or counterfeit.

Let he who is without sin cast the first stone. Please do not make judgments about altars until you have first sought God to reveal impurity in your own life. Then and only then can you become part of the answer, rather than increasing the problem. God gives grace for ministers to develop. Never try to bring a correction that is heavier than the bridge of relationship can bear. All bridges are weight rated for maximum load. Relationships are like bridges into the hearts of individuals. You cannot drive a ten-ton correction over a one-ton bridge of relationship. You will crash every time and you will insulate the person further so that to hear and accept the same correction now requires a fifteen-ton bridge of relationship. The prophetic price for bringing a correction often includes paying the price to love people long enough to build a ten-ton bridge of relationship so we can bring a ten-ton correction that is heard and then hopefully accepted!

There's a transfer of wealth
That soon is to come,
A great harvest awaits
Untold souls to be won.

Have our "tithe-traditions"
Left us on shaky ground,
Saints, God's truth on the tithe
In His Word will be found.

Come kneel at pure altars
Dip hearts fully clean,
With resources released
May this harvest Christ glean.

CHAPTER 11

SEEING GOD

Blessed are the pure in heart, for they shall see God.
— Matthew 5:8

The apostolic understanding of this beatitude is perhaps best expressed in Hebrews 12:14:

Make every effort to live in peace with all men and to be holy. Without holiness no one will see the Lord.

At the risk of sounding theological, I want to quote one of the finest statements I have ever read concerning the single thread of both Matthew 5:8 and Hebrews 12:14. *The Expositor's Greek Testament* says of the promise of Matthew 5:8:[14]

---

14. Biblical definitions from Alexander Balmon Bruce, D.D., *The Expositor's Greek Testament,* edited by W. Robertson Nicoll, M.A., LL.D. Vol. I. Copyright 1983 (Wm. B. Eerdmans Publishing Co., 255 Jefferson SE, Grand Rapids, MI 49503), p. 122.

"shall see God": **ton the-on ops-on-tai:** their reward is the beatific vision. Some think the reference is not to the faculty of clear vision but to the rare privilege of seeing the face of the great King (so Fritzsche and Schange). "The expression has its origin in the ways of Eastern monarchs, who rarely show themselves in public, so that only the most intimate circle behold the royal countenance" (Schanz) = the **pure** have **access** to **the all** but inaccessible. (Emphasis is author's.)

I love the statement, "Only the most intimate circle behold the royal countenance." On one side of the theological balance scales, this thought offers a concrete "Armenian" reason why some are seeing God in action while others are not. On the other side of the scales, the reason is God's sovereign choice.

There was a distinct difference between the ministry of Jesus and that of the scribes and Pharisees. The ministry of the apostles was recognizably different from that of the chief priests and elders of Israel. How much of that difference do we attribute to sovereignty and how much to obedience?

God made it possible for the people to clearly distinguish between those serving dead tradition and those serving the living God. You could easily *see* the difference. In John 14 (NIV), Philip asked, "Lord, show us the Father and that will be enough for us."

Jesus answered in verses 9–12:

> *Don't you know me, Philip, even after I have been among you such a long time? Anyone who has seen me has seen the Father. How can you say, 'Show us the Father?' Don't you believe that I am in the Father, and that the Father is in me? The words I say to you are not just my own. Rather, it is the Father living in me, who is doing his work. Believe me when I say that I am in the Father and the Father is in me; or at*

least believe on the evidence of the miracles themselves. I tell you the truth, anyone who has faith in me will do what I have been doing. He will do even greater things than these, because I am going to the Father.

Blueprint for Ministry

There was never a sharper blueprint for ministry than what we see here. Jesus made it very clear to the disciples that His mission was to demonstrate God. If He obeyed the leadership of the Holy Spirit, people would see God. That was not just a one-time statement about His personal life, but a principle which would effectively govern ministry. The church should be demonstrating the Father. Unbelievers should see God working and living through us. What was the difference between Jesus and the scribes and Pharisees? He taught and ministered *as one who had authority.* Demons were subject to Him. Sickness and disease had to bow and flee at His command.

We live in a dying world that is filled with unbelievers. Some are going to hell because, instead of seeing God in us, they see church competition, misappropriation of funds, begging for finances on television and radio, manipulation, selling, profiteering from the gospel, and believers suing each other in court. We are called to demonstrate God's authority in the earth. Jesus made this very clear in John 14:12, ". . . he who believes in Me, the works that I do he will do also. . . ."

The world will see God operating in the church when purification comes to our altars. *Our effectiveness in spiritual things is determined by the purity of our hearts before God.* The Word ministered or shared out of a pure heart comes forth with clarity and impact that can be achieved no other way. The prayer prayed by the leadership of the Spirit out of a pure heart is assured an answer. John 14:13–14 (NIV) says:

And I will do whatever you ask in my name, so that the Son may bring glory to the Father. You may ask me for anything in my name, and I will do it.

Many prayers are prayed that do not receive answers. Could it be because they are prayed out of something less than a pure heart?

A Righteous Gentile Is Honored

Cornelius is an example of a man who was visited supernaturally. The Bible is not silent about why. What he did came from a pure heart. Both his prayers and his giving came before God as a memorial, which shows us that whenever something comes out of a pure heart, God notices, hears, and responds accordingly.

An angel was dispatched to Cornelius with very specific instructions. He was told to contact Peter, and he was given detailed instructions on how to find the house where Peter was staying.

Just as the visit to Cornelius was supernatural, so was God's moving on Peter to prepare him to step beyond tradition and minister to the Gentiles. When Cornelius' messengers arrived, Peter was ready to accompany them because God had given him the same vision three times.

The Holy Spirit even told Peter that three men were looking for him and without hesitating to go downstairs and go with them for "I have sent them." Why did God choose Cornelius for a mighty visitation and to be the first Gentile filled with the Holy Spirit? Do you suppose it was because of his pure heart? How many people will God use us to bring into the Kingdom if we will but walk before Him in purity. If we allow the Holy Spirit to purify us through His revealed Word, we can expect to see God in manifestation through us.

What Financial Pressure Reveals

This seems to be a season in the Body of Christ when many are under financial pressure. If we point our finger at impurity in our corporate altars as the sole reason, we will greatly err. We should *first* look in the mirror and ask God if perhaps He is trying to reveal the effects of the spirit of mammon at work in our individual lives.

Different gospels record Jesus addressing this issue: *"You cannot serve God and money."* How much trust have we put in the material things of this world? Our culture is shot through with materialism, and often it seems the spirit of mammon dominates the desires of God's people. When financial pressure arises, we are confronted with our own lusts, wrong desires, and undetected trust in material things. It is painful when God deals with us in this way, but it certainly is effective!

Financial pressure can quickly reveal heart attitude. We can learn that the things we thought were necessary for our well-being and happiness are not needed at all. The spirit of mammon has some unique manifestations which need to be considered. It can cause an individual to give for the wrong reasons and to give to the wrong place without seeking God's wisdom or direction. It usually manifests itself through impure motivation.

It seems at times people are trying to manipulate God through giving. We do that by *giving in order to get.* Our reasoning generally misapplies some of the things we have been taught. We find the promise of a thirty, sixty, and hundredfold return, so we begin to give with a motivation for a thirty, sixty or hundredfold return. Soon we find ourselves giving in order to receive, with help from ministries promising thirty, sixty or a hundredfold if we give to them. "I will give so much into this ministry, and I am claiming a certain return; therefore, I can expect God to give me back a certain amount, or to give me what I need." There is a difference in giving by faith in God's promises and giving by obedience to His prompting.

Giving by faith in response to biblical promises and admonitions like Proverbs 19:17, "He who has pity on the poor lends to the LORD, And He will pay back what he has given" is always good. The problem with this giving is that it can be subject to manipulation when the Word is used by the unscrupulous. Luke 6:38 can be quoted in an appeal quite effectively: "Give, and it will be given to you: good measure, pressed down, shaken together, and running over will be put into your bosom. For with the same measure that you use, it will be measured back to you." Good-hearted people often succumb to this manipulation.

If we condition ourselves to give only at the prompting of the Holy Spirit, we protect our hearts from the manipulators. When the one-hundredfold appears in Scripture, it is the result of Holy Spirit obedience. Isaac refused to reproduce Abram's failure of going to Egypt. He stayed and obeyed by sowing during famine. I see no guarantee of a hundredfold in sowing "by faith" as manipulators often promise but only by obedience—wait for God's leading. Refuse to be manipulated by the ministerial mammonites.

God does promise that He will give back to us, but there is a heart attitude which must reflect His. If we look at Jesus as the example, John 3:16 says, "God so **loved** that He gave. . . ." Ephesians 5 says we are to ". . . imitate God as well beloved children imitate their father."

The motivation of God's heart for giving Jesus was love. If our giving comes out of a pure heart, we can certainly expect a return. But have we crossed the line? Are we subtly giving because we want a specific return? We need to examine our motivation for giving. Some people who are wealthy give with the intention of exerting control over church leaders. This financial pressure can be applied in a variety of ways to influence decisions made concerning the church or ministry.

Giving With Strings Attached

I attended a church with a wealthy man who loved to sing out of a hymnal, but the worship leader only used spontaneous songs in praise and worship. This contemporary style of praise and worship violated the rich man's favorite tradition. He promised to give the church a large sum if they would buy his favorite hymnals.

What pastor could pass up a $100,000 gift, especially when they only had to spend a small percentage to satisfy the giver? The motivation for the giving was obvious. The problem was, the leadership needed the money. They began to reason, "What can it hurt? Let's go ahead and buy the hymnals. We do not have to use them very often." But when somebody gives $100,000 to your church for buying hymnals, you'd better believe there will be pressure to use them.

There is certainly nothing wrong with hymnals. This is just one example of how manipulation can motivate giving. Those of us who stand in leadership positions really need to seek God for wisdom as to how to handle such situations. Receiving money into our ministry tainted by impure motivation can bring impurity into the corporate altar.

Another form of manipulation comes through people who are helped through a ministry. They decide that the pastor or the prayer team, rather than the grace of God, is responsible for their blessing. They continue to give solely with the expectation, hope, and sometimes pressure, for church leadership to do their personal spiritual warfare. In effect, they are buying your prayer time for them. At that point, if a leader continues to receive their money, it is no longer the Holy Spirit who is guiding the prayer time, but an obligation to pray consistently for the one who is giving!

I know of one pastor who was told by the Holy Spirit that his church could not keep any of the money given by a person over a period of time. He was instructed to give all the money back. The pastor said, "Because the money was given out of a wrong motive, we could not keep any of it in the ministry. Any of the money kept would have had a polluting effect upon the ministry." The Holy Spirit is our guide. The concept of the "Anointing to Spoil" as practiced financially in Scripture redeems the money taken through warfare and sanctifies it in its use when spent for Kingdom purposes. Isaiah says in the last days that God will anoint businesses for this purpose.

If a mafia leader or drug dealer were to find salvation and give part of their ill-gotten gain, would it be acceptable? The answer is in our relationship with the Holy Spirit. If some of it is "blood money" then it must be prayed over. Even Judas' thirty pieces of silver was redeemed by buying a "Potter's field" but because it was blood money it had to be treated differently. The end-time prophetic concept of the "Anointing to Spoil" as executed by the church is a judgment on the spirit of mammon, taking money from the world and using it to disciple nations.

Some people give into ministries in order to be noticed and considered for leadership positions. The deacon's ministry has probably been bought more than any other. Sometimes the motivation is ambition, other times, recognition or the desire to have an opportunity to minister. There are many great promises of God that show us His desire to multiply and return what we give. Nevertheless, we really need to check our hearts and make sure our motivation is pure. Then and only then are we going to see the Lord move in the financial realm. Isaiah prophesied we would see Him!

Some people come under financial pressure simply because of disobedience. We cannot go out and blindly buy everything we want and expect God to bless it. We are really servants of the Lord, and we must submit our decisions to the Holy Spirit. When we buy things we want, but God has not instructed us to get, He has no obligation to pay for them.

When I was in seminary, one of the things we were taught which made a strong impression on me was, "What God tells you to do, *He* pays for. What you decide to do on your own, *you* pay for." I have met many people in the Body of Christ who are under financial pressure strictly because of what they did apart from God. Usually large items are involved, such as a house, car, recreational vehicle, boat, or something else which was not necessarily needed.

How and When to Receive

Manipulation is as dangerous as disobedience. As I was finishing the first half of this book and getting ready for a trip to the Midwest, our air-conditioner went out the day before I left. During the course of doing local Bible studies every week for twelve years, I had met a wonderful Christian family whose business was air-conditioning. I called the man and he agreed to drop by my house and look over the unit. I knew it needed to be replaced because of some previous work.

The next day I left for the Midwest with the understanding that it was to be replaced with one of equal capacity. He replaced both heating and air-conditioning units, and when I got home I called him to get the cost. He said he and his wife had prayed about it, and decided they wanted to give the unit into our ministry.

In the first place, they would not have been giving it to the ministry; they would have been giving it to me personally. Second, I did not feel in my heart I could accept that gift. The reason was that I had initiated the contact. Had the Holy Spirit initiated the chain of events, then I could have received it. Had that man called me by the leadership of the Holy Spirit and said, "The Lord told me you need a new heating and air-conditioning unit, and I am supposed to give it to you," then I could have received it. But because I called him and asked him to come out and look at the unit, I was the one who initiated the activity. Therefore, to have received it from him would have been to take advantage of a good-hearted brother, which is all too common in ministry!

When I shared that principle with him on the phone, he related to me two incidents where he felt advantage had been taken. He was overjoyed at my stand. His business activity had been down, and he really did not feel like he could afford to do that for me, yet he and his wife wanted to bless me with all their heart. Those of us in leadership need to realize that the saints long to bless and give to us, but there is a standard of integrity that we need to raise up concerning how we deal with the people to whom we minister.

I want to see God in my life and ministry. I know for that to happen, I must maintain a level of integrity where my own heart does not in any way condemn me when I go before Him in prayer. When I pray from a pure foundation, I know I am going to receive what I am asking for, as long as I am asking in the will of the Father.

The reason I could turn down the offer for the heating and airconditioning unit was because of a much smaller incident that happened early in my ministry. There was a man attending my Bible studies who owned an auto parts store. I needed a battery at one point, so I decided to give him the business. I went into his store and got the battery I needed, and in the process he said, "I want to give you this battery." I told him I wanted to pay for it, but he said, "No, I want to give you this battery." So I took the battery, even though I had gone to see him to buy one.

The Disappearing Donor

After about two weeks, I never saw that man again in my Bible study. As I prayed about the situation, I felt like the Lord showed me that this man began to look at me as falling into a common category with so many others, willing to take advantage of any situation. At that point, I began to pray about God's necessary standard for dealing with saints who own their own businesses.

I believe integrity demands that what we, as ministers of the gospel, initiate with Christian brothers and sisters in business, we pay for. When the Holy Spirit initiates something, however, what they want to give can be received with rejoicing and thanksgiving. But when we initiate the contact with Christian business people, it is incumbent upon us to pay for what we get. Only then are there good feelings on both sides, and when the day comes we need their services again, we can ask with a clear conscience. "Blessed are the pure in heart, for they shall see God" (Matthew 5:8). Jesus said, "The works that I do he will do also; and greater works than these he will do because I go to My Father" (John 14:12).

I believe we are rapidly approaching a season when God demands to be seen in the lives of every believer. The key to God's being seen is clear. It requires purity of heart, motivation, thought, and action. Hebrews 14:16 says we can ". . . come boldly to the throne of grace, that we may obtain mercy and find grace to help in time of need." We need to remember ". . . that only the most intimate circle behold the royal countenance. The pure have access to the all but inaccessible."

As the Lord leads us to ever-greater heights of purity and accountability, we can expect His visible manifestation. Multitudes of unbelievers will have to acknowledge they *see* God at work in the church. Then and only then will the great end-time harvest come forth.

Once again, God is waiting on us!

Is climbing the ladder
Your heart motivation,
Or is serving others
What brings inspiration?

No position, prestige
Or power can compare,
With being Christlike
Holy Spirit aware.

PART II

PURIFYING THE PERSONAL ALTAR

CHAPTER 12

PURIFYING THE HEART "MOTIVATION"

Hebrews 11:8–9 says,

> *By faith Abraham obeyed when he was called to go out to the place which he would afterward receive as an inheritance. And he went out, not knowing where he was going. By faith he sojourned in the land of promise as in a foreign country, dwelling in tents with Isaac and Jacob, the heirs with him of the same promise; for he waited. . . .*

Are we willing to wait? Abraham waited. For what did he wait? ". . . for the city which has foundations. . . ." There are a variety of spiritual cities being built today with persuasive appeals to participate. Apostolic networks abound, but what is the condition of the altar? The foundation of any altar has to begin with the cross. The willingness to apply the cross demonstrates a foundation built on something other than self. Wisdom dictates that we refrain from covenanting with people before walking through enough adversity to reveal the depth of the cross embraced. The application of the cross often reveals lapses in character development. If we choose to faithfully repeat what we hear God saying, then the consequences in today's culture do not favor quick growth or a large church. It sometimes seems a false prophet is much more likely to have a large church than a true one. When God builds a city, the foundation is His unadulterated Word. If a church grows large by adulterating the Word, and choosing a ministry philosophy which constantly neglects any passages that address sin, then what is our condition after participating with that defilement? Ancient wine merchants adulterated wine by "watering it down." God's Word can be adulterated the same way. Paul refers to this common practice in 2 Corinthians 2:15–17:

> *For we are to God the fragrance of Christ among those who are being saved and among those who are perishing. To the one we are the aroma of death to death, and to the other the aroma of life to life. And who is sufficient for these things? For we are not, as so many, peddling the word of God; but as of sincerity, but as from God, we speak in the sight of God in Christ."*

The Greek word translated peddling is **kap-ale-yoo-o** meaning to adulterate or dilute for profit. Even the apostle Paul confronted seeker-sensitive Christianity. In our rush to make church a friendly place, we can now offer Bud Lite, Miller Lite and Christianity Lite—all with half the calories. If we choose to join such an altar, the best that can be said is that we are half-fed.

In 1986, the Lord spoke to me in my prayer closet. This was the second time I had heard one of those "thundering voices on the inside" that cause you to look around to see if God is in the room sitting behind you. The first occurrence was when He called me into the ministry. This was the second. It was so loud it had to be audible. It was emphatic. It was exclamatory. It sounded like thunder. He said, "Prepare My people for persecution." I studied but could not find much initially and finally cobbled together a four-message series based on what little I found. It was so well received that it inspired a permanent fifty percent reduction in Bible study attendance. It was my first revelation of what happens when you get a word from the Lord that people do not want to hear. In street language, the believers pulled what is called a "splitzo-supremo, adios amigo, don't call us, we'll call you." If we are truly prophetic, God will faithfully continue the process of giving us unwelcomed words until the unwelcomed looks do not bother us. Ezekiel's bronze forehead will be reproduced in end-time prophets.

Fifteen years later, I published the book *Marked Men*. The book was delivered to our office on 9-11, the same day the World Trade Center was destroyed. What God spoke about audibly revealed a primary foundation. The subject was the necessity of preparing now for coming persecution. Jesus prepared the Twelve for the persecution their generation would encounter. Many churches today want the same level of anointing as the early church without the preparational price. What is wrong with this picture? Will God honor our promise of end-time anointing without early church dedication?

The end-time church cannot expect the fullness of God's anointing if the ministers are not willing to preach all of God's Word. Removing the confrontational passages by refusing to even read them fails the most basic smell test for the gospel. Let not the doubleminded man think he will receive anything from the Lord. What kind of church do we want? A peaceful, easygoing safe place where mush and milk-toast prevail cannot prepare us for what is ahead. We face the opposite of the church Jesus experienced in Matthew 23:4–6:

For they bind heavy burdens, hard to bear, and lay them on men's shoulders; but they themselves will not move them with one of their fingers. But all their works they do to be seen by men. They make their phylacteries broad and enlarge the borders of their garments. They love the best places at feasts, the best seats in the synagogues. . . .

What kind of church does this describe? The church today has removed all demands, even holiness, and still expects the blessing of God. We are looking at an organization that is political. Political positioning defiles an altar by idolatry. Can growth become an idol and defile an altar? If we choose to avoid preaching anything controversial to keep people, we have bowed the knee and worshipped a foreign god, defiling the altar. Any church refusing to state what God says about any issue, for fear of offending people, is an impure altar masquerading as a house of God. It is probably a house of gold. When a preacher becomes a master of mammon, he is worthless for ever preparing people to walk through the end-times or meeting Jesus!

Jesus said of leaders in Matthew 23:6–10:

They love the best places at feasts, the best seats in the synagogues, greetings in the marketplaces, and to be called by men, "Rabbi, Rabbi." But you, do not be called "Rabbi" for One is your Teacher, the Christ, and you are all brethren. Do not call anyone on earth your father; for One is your Father, He who is in heaven. And do not be called teachers; for One is your Teacher, the Christ.

Why have many apostolic networks folded or been disbanded? Three defiling categories bring judgment: spiritual politics, mammon and failure to serve. When organizations offer special privileges based on the size of a ministry, they usually insulate against purity. **Selling Fatherhood** at five percent or ten percent a month would make Peter and Paul vomit. Unadulterated apostolic fatherhood gives or lays up for the children. It does not charge them. The fastest way to forfeit a fathering anointing is to sell it. Selling the anointing makes leaders spiritual pimps. Any organization whose members serve *it* more than *it* serves its members has a structural spiritual problem, foundational in nature, that could and should end its life.

Jesus was not kidding when He said in verse 11, "But he who is greatest among you shall be your servant." Altars quickly get defiled when servanthood is perverted or cast aside. How can any man of God retreat from moral leadership, refuse to confront sin and still call it church? The lie must be "If I major in love, grace and mercy, more people will come and eventually get saved." That reasoning is suited for a "man of gold" but not a "man of God." Jesus did not say in the great commission, "Go make converts." He said, "Make disciples." A watered-down weasel's gospel produces a spineless church incapable of confronting the power of darkness currently inundating the land. (See *Converts or Disciples? A Prophetic Word to the American Church*.)

Verses 11–14 say:

> . . . *he who is greatest among you shall be your servant. And whoever exalts himself will be abased, and he who humbles himself will be exalted. But woe to you, scribes and Pharisees, hypocrites. For you shut up the kingdom of heaven against men; for you neither go in yourselves, nor do you allow those who are entering to go in. Woe to you, scribes and Pharisees, hypocrites. For you devour widows' houses, and for a pretense make long prayers. Therefore you will receive greater condemnation.*

I always wondered how the leaders of Jesus' day ". . . devoured widows' houses. . . .."? The puzzle pieces did not fall together until verse 19 where God commands us to maintain a pure altar. When we maintain a pure altar, all the giving deposited there is sanctified, **hagee-ad-zo**, and receives covenantal blessing. But if we do not maintain a pure altar, the covenant does not work and those people who most need a return are not covenantally guaranteed one except by grace. The widow's mite, which desperately needs to be blessed, becomes defiled. That issue alone demands judgment on the perpetrators.

Verses 15–19 say:

Woe to you, scribes and Pharisees, hypocrites. For you travel land and sea to win one proselyte and when he is won, you make him twice as much a son of hell as yourselves. Woe to you, blind guides, who say, "Whoever swears by the temple, it is nothing; but whoever swears by the gold of the temple, he is obliged to perform it." Fools and blind. For which is greater, the gold or the temple that sanctifies the gold? And, "Whoever swears by the altar, it is nothing; but whoever swears by the gift that is on it, he is obliged to perform it." Fools and blind. For which is greater, the gift or the altar that sanctifies the gift?

The Spirit of Balaam at Work

Pure altars release blessing. Defiled altars demand judgment. Let's suppose I attend a church whose pastor, priest or bishop has endorsed same-sex marriage or homosexual ordination. The defilement of that altar by sexual perversion has spiritual authority to attack me and my family, if I associate with it. If I give to that altar, my giving unites me with the altar and what should dispense covenantal blessing now delivers spiritual perversion. Not only am I cut off from covenant blessing, but by association, partake of another's sin. Second John, verse 11, warns about partaking of another's sins through a greeting—how much more by giving?

The homosexual community should be welcomed at our altars to find deliverance. If we turn what God ordained as a place of deliverance into a place, that through deception deepens the darkness, we transfer our eternal destiny to the deepest darkest regions of the damned. Any congregation whose bishop or denomination chooses to ordain a homosexual priest should immediately cut off all money or risk the assault of perverse spirits on their families. Why would any Christian subject their children to homosexuality by giving into such an altar? That qualifies spiritually as brain-dead and stupid, rebellious behavior. Are God's people destroyed for a lack of knowledge? What pastor in his right mind wants to give an account for defiling families? "Depart from me you worker of iniquity, I never knew you" may be a familiar refrain on Judgment Day for many church leaders. Do not allow the perversion of one man like a bishop to destroy your family. Cut off all giving to any group who continues to participate with those who ordain and promote perversion. Why should the hell they have chosen come upon you? The altar sanctifies the gift and leaders are responsible for the condition of the altar.

One really good question at this point is, "Would God ever lead a believer to continue giving to an impure altar?" While speculating on what God might or might not do is always dangerous, I would strongly lean toward saying, "No, unless He is filling the cup of iniquity for judgment." The possible parallel pattern for what God might do comes from the sons of Eli, who defiled their altars much like today's priests who approve and practice homosexual marriage. First Samuel 2:22–25 states,

> *Now Eli was very old; and he heard everything his sons did to all Israel, and how they lay with the women who assembled*

at the door of the tabernacle of meetings. So he said to them, 'Why do you do such things? For I hear of your evil dealings from all the people. No, my sons. For it is not a good report that I hear. You make the LORD'S people transgress. If one man sins against another, God will judge him. But if a man sins against the LORD, who will intercede for him?' Nevertheless they did not heed the voice of their father, because **the LORD desired to kill them**.

Eli's sons refused to hear his correction—because God sought to kill them, because their sin was so grievous. The one reason God might lead you to continue giving to an impure altar is the principle of "fullness of iniquity" where you would be expediting judgment. (For a complete explanation of "fullness," see *Marked Men*). Another reason God might lead you to continue giving is the covenantal right to pray imprecatory prayers demanding judgment on the offending party (see *The Sure Mercies of David—Part II*). Ananias and Sapphira events are coming. The candidates are lining up. The majority of those candidates seem to be occupying pulpits rather than sitting in the pew. Let the intercessors expedite the manifestation!

The Altar of the Heart

Just as the pastoral leadership team has a covenantal responsibility to keep the altar pure for the sake of the people, so does each individual have a covenantal obligation to keep their relationship free from defiling judgments and strife. The Sermon on the Mount was not delivered to the multitude, but to the disciples and could be viewed as ministry marching orders. Matthew 5:23–24 states:

Therefore if you bring your gift to the altar, and there remember that your brother has something against you, leave your gift there before the altar, and go your way, First be reconciled to your brother, and then come and offer your gift.

It is not enough to attend a pure altar; we have an individual obligation to keep our personal altar pure. Relationships, when broken, can hinder God's provision. The prevailing question is how do we "ferret out" these hidden issues that hinder covenant promises? The beginning of an answer emerges in Luke 22:10–12 in how they found the upper room:

> *And He said to them, "Behold, when you have entered the city, a man will meet you carrying a pitcher of water; follow him into the house which he enters. Then you shall say to the master of the house, 'The Teacher says to you, "Where is the guest room in which I may eat the Passover with My disciples?"' Then he will show you a large, furnished upper room; there make ready."*

The issue is that God is faithful to reveal offenses when we ask. He will open wounds that they may be healed. God has divine appointments which are usually concealed in hidden places. Often the greatest work that God does comes when we allow the Holy Spirit to lead us, finding eternal gold in hidden places. It is not advertised. It is not something that everybody knows. It comes by a manifestation of the leadership of the Holy Spirit. I would have never found the truth on the altar had I not, years ago, allowed the Lord through some divine appointments to radically redirect my course. Changing course is costly when it closes nearly all ministry doors. When I first published *Purifying the Altar*, it closed nearly every ministry door in California. Those were very tough years.

This is a season for showing foundations. God is laying foundations on the inside of us—foundations that will carry us, I trust, through this next season, the great harvest and the winding up of the age. The issue becomes, are we willing to let the Lord take us into His secret place and do the work He wants to do? God has individual secret rooms of preparation. We can choose to build our own city or we can submit to the Holy Spirit pursuing the one for which Abraham was looking. Every one of the Twelve whom Jesus called had a foundation from a religious city which had to be replaced because it was crooked, warped and/or dysfunctional. God always starts with foundational issues. Jesus dealt with foundational issues from the call of the Twelve through the Last Supper.

Luke 22:14–16 says:

And when the hour had come, He sat down, and the twelve apostles with Him. Then He said to them, "With fervent desire I have desired to eat this Passover with you before I suffer; for I say to you, I will no longer eat of it until it is fulfilled in the kingdom of God."

When we read verses 14–20, we ask what was behind the *"fervent desire"* to eat the Passover before He suffered. What unaccomplished goal yet remained after three and one half years? The gospel of John allots five chapters to what Luke covers in a few verses. John's account may shed light on the *"fervent desire."* Each of the five chapters portray significant life-changing messages which were essential for the foundational formation of the early church. A quick synopsis of major themes in each chapter follows: John 13 accentuates servanthood by example with foot washing. John 14 says, "In My Father's house are many **mon-ay**, places of ministry, so you don't have to fight over who is the greatest." "We will come to you and make our abode with you"; John 15 says, "You have not chosen Me, but I have chosen you and ordained you"; John 16 says, "I will give you another Comforter"; John 17 says in the High Priestly prayer of Jesus, "The glory You have given Me, I have given them." This was probably the most significant encounter that Jesus had with the Twelve in all three and a half years. It took place at the end of His life and summarizes His ministry. This is why He ". . . *fervently desired*. . ." a final preparational input. The same *"fervent desire"* Jesus had for the Twelve, I believe He has for our preparation at the end of the age. There is an appointed season and an appointed place for the revelation of heart issues. It is inner man impartation. It goes to the depth and core of our being where only spiritual surgery works. He is standing at the door, for some of us, without anesthesia.

John 22:19–22 says:

And He took bread, gave thanks and broke it, and gave it to them, saying, 'This is My body which is given for you; do this in remembrance of Me.' Likewise He also took the cup after supper, saying, "This cup is the new covenant of My blood, which is shed for you. But behold, the hand of My betrayer is with Me on the table. And truly the Son of Man goes as it has been determined, but woe to that man by whom He is betrayed!"

For three and a half years, Jesus had dealt with disciples competing for position. Peter, James and John emerged as chief leaders probably from participation in events like the Transfiguration. The competition-driven strife was disqualifying them for ministry and had to be confronted.

Verse 23 of Luke 22, says, "Then they began to question among themselves, which of them it was who would do this thing. But there was also rivalry among them. . . ." Competition for position killed all discernment of the betrayal in their midst.

Jesus did not have any trouble discerning the betrayal. God has called us to be a prophetic people. Why don't we discern betrayal and diminish the damage? There are costly reasons why we fail to discern. The Twelve needed spiritual heart surgery. Without the surgery, heart issues have a blinding effect. If we are willing to submit to the process, discernment can be recovered. What produces betrayal in leadership, whether in church or business? Selfish ambition is usually the motivational culprit pushing one individual ahead of others!

A different kind of servanthood emerged for me in 1985 when the Lord led me into a policy that would last for twenty-one years of "no longer selling books and tapes." I did not have any idea what the fruit of "Pray and Obey" would be. I had a choice: to obey or to disobey. I initially promised only one year because of my ministry track record. Experience revealed some thirty percent of the budget coming in from the book and tape table and I calculated if that revenue was lost we would not have been able to pay the bills. So in 1985, I agreed to "one year." What I did not calculate was the heart surgery over the spirit of mammon. God began to reveal to me issues that were killing my discernment.

The first step for me was blind obedience to the Lord's direction, not knowing if we would survive financially. The fruit of obedience was spiritual clarity which in some ways is still happening. Some revelation comes by grace corresponding to a five-fold gift like teaching, but others from sheer obedience. I am still reaping the blessing of obedience from a decision I made in December of 1984. When God comes to us and says there is a foundational brick He wants to put in our lives—we must accept. Often we do not realize it is foundational. We do not see it the same way God does. He just comes and says, "I want you to do this" and everything in our flesh says, "No, I do not want to do this." I thought, "This will not work. I am going to take one year and prove that it does not work." What is the difference between this kind of refusal and Peter rebuking Jesus when He said He was going to the cross? There is not much difference. How many of us learn like Peter? I do not mind learning like Peter if it leads to Acts 5 power where our shadow heals.

> *But there was rivalry among them, as to which of them should be considered the greatest. And He said to them, "The kings of the Gentiles exercise lordship over them, and those who exercise authority over them are called "benefactors." But not so among you. . . ."*
>
> —Luke 22:24–26a

God had switched my ministry paradigm and I did not even know it. The world uses faith to extract what they want (usually money) by making people believe they need a product (marketing). When ministers use the same methodology and promote with a motivation to sell their anointing, Satan receives it as worship. I was dragged kicking and screaming into servanthood. In the new paradigm, I found myself using my faith to extract from God what people needed and giving it to them on a "Pray and Obey" basis.

> *. . . But not so among you; on the contrary, he who is chief/greatest* **[hayg-eh-om-ahee/hegeomai]** *among you, let him be as the younger, and he who governs as he who serves. For who is greater, he who sits at the table, or he who serves? Is it not he who sits at the table? Yet I am among you as the One who serves.*
>
> —Luke 26b–27

The desire to govern, to lead, to preside, to rule, to gain honor, to have fame and money is so great, it motivates many. In this arena, there is little difference between the church and the world. The only way to build a giant apostolic Burger Chain is to sell the anointing. Such behavior motivated the Savior to clean house in the Temple. In 2 Corinthians 2:17, Paul considered such activity as utterly defiling. In Acts 8:22, Peter was not sure one could be saved after sinking so low.

Now contrast that with Philippians 2:1–7:

> *Therefore if there is any consolation in Christ, if any comfort of love, if any fellowship of the Spirit, if any affection and mercy, fulfill my joy by being* **phro-neh-o***/like-minded, having the same love, being of one accord, of one* **phro-neho***/mind. Let nothing be done through selfish ambition or conceit, but in lowliness of mind let each* **hayg-eh-om-ahee / hegeomai** *esteem others better than himself.*

What was happening with the Twelve is happening today. "But there was a rivalry/strife among them as to . . ." who was most "esteemed." "Pray and Obey" killed all desire to go to large churches or do TV, because of the expense of material taken. Any kind of national exposure would have bankrupted the ministry. One quick move on God's part resulted in heart surgery. God will test whom we serve—self or others. Which choice will we make? Am I going to live for pushing me up the ladder or am I going to live for serving others? That is the root contrast between these two systems. As a minister, the choices I make determine whether I embrace the cross or reject it. By using faith to recruit churches and extract a monthly percentage for an apostolic fatherly covering, I potentially join the counterfeit apostles. Paul identified this group in 2 Corinthians 11:7–12, vowing to continue to make the gospel free so the church could see the difference. Verses 7–12 say:

Did I commit sin in abasing myself that you might be exalted, because I preached the gospel of God to you free of charge? I robbed other churches, taking wages from them to minister to you. And when I was present with you, and in need, I was a burden to no one, for what was lacking to me the brethren who came from Macedonia supplied. And in everything I kept myself from being burdensome to you, and so I will keep myself. As the truth of Christ is in me, no one shall stop me from this boasting in the regions of Achaia. Why? Because I do not love you? God knows. But what I do, I will also continue to do, that I may cut off the opportunity from those who desire an opportunity to be regarded just as we are in the things of which they boast.

Verses 4–9 say:

*Let each of you look out not only for his own interests, but also for the interests of others. Let this **phro-neh-o**/attitude be in you which was also in Christ Jesus, who, being in the form of God, did not consider it robbery to be equal with God, but made Himself of no reputation, taking the form of a servant, and coming in the likeness of men. And being found in appearance as a man, He humbled Himself and became obedient to the point of death, even the death of the cross. Therefore God also has highly exalted Him. . . .*

Can you imagine being the wealthiest person in the world and setting it all aside to go serve others by being their steward or housecleaner? God knows how to develop servanthood. Why is it that Jesus said to the rich young ruler, "It's very hard for a rich man to come into the kingdom of God"? What was that bridge they had difficulty crossing? Can we imagine today's wealthiest giving everything away to serve others? Imagine America's wealthiest corporate head coming to mow your yard or clean your house. What is the issue? The issue is heart motivation. God values servanthood while we value accomplishment. It takes an attitude adjustment. The attitude that Jesus demonstrated is what God has to birth in us. Choosing the cross is never easy, but it always has eternal rewards.

Now this same word **hayg-eh-om-ahee/hegeomai** appears in Hebrews 11. Every one of the Twelve wanted to be chief, taking over when Jesus departed. Hebrews 11:24 says, "By faith Moses, when he became of age, refused to be called the son of Pharaoh's daughter, choosing rather to suffer affliction with the people of God than to enjoy the passing pleasures of sin. . . ." This was a very Christlike choice. Moses, as a member of Pharaoh's house, had access to everything he could ever want, but chose to give it up. It is the call of a servant that comes on our life for God's purposes in our generation.

Verse 26 says, "**hayg-eh-om-ahee/hegeomai**/esteeming. . . ." Moses made a choice that the Twelve refused for three and a half years. The Twelve were **esteeming** position not to serve but to rule, expecting to profit from the position. Position, prestige and power *here* cannot compare to ". . . well done good and faithful . . ." *there*. The apostles wanted the security of being the leader. Moses chose a different realm using a different yardstick ". . . esteeming the reproach of Christ." Reasoning this way requires a transition in the heart—a transition only God can accomplish. What person, in their right mind looks for the ". . . reproach of Christ"? Who can see it as ". . . greater riches than the treasures in Egypt"? What was the ". . . reward"? The reward was preparing the heart to fulfill God's call regardless of the price. The heart of a servant is necessary to carry God's anointing successfully. Without that heart, the danger of abusing our God-given authority is real and the consequences are usually eternal. Moses developed a relationship with God that resulted in delivering a nation from captivity. His enemies were another matter—the earth separated to swallow them alive. This level of relationship is necessary to wind up the age.

Jesus mentions the reward for serving in Luke 22:28:

But you are those who have continued with Me in My trials. And I bestow upon you a kingdom, just as My Father bestowed one upon Me, that you may eat and drink at My table in My kingdom, and sit on thrones judging the twelve tribes of Israel.

There is a picture here. Servanthood + obedience + continued faithfulness = authority. God's preparational pathway has a reward: Spiritual Judicial Authority.

Verse 31 says, "And the Lord said, 'Simon, Simon. Indeed, Satan has ("demanded" NAS) permission to sift you like wheat." The Greek word has the authority of *"demanded."* The early church experienced the awesome miraculous power of God but their preparation included demoralizing failure. Peter denied Jesus three times and the others hid in fear of losing their lives. Personal failure had a wonderful humbling affect which seems to have helped in the preparational process. The magnitude of the call for some seems to determine the magnitude of testing. To the degree that God has chosen you to make inroads into the kingdom of darkness seems to parallel the degree to which the enemy has the legal right to test you. And notice—it was given to him. ". . . that he may sift you as wheat. But I have prayed for you, that your faith should not fail; and when you have returned to Me, strengthen your brethren." Peter's failure was preparational. God redeemed the failure. Do we view failures as preparational? (See *The Sure Mercies of David—Part I.*)

God's definition of failure and ours are often two very different things. God does not necessarily define failure as sin. Failure would much more likely be defined as imminent when there was a refusal to turn, **ep-ee-stref-o** or repent. When does God count a man or a woman to be in failure? When they refuse to turn and deal with their issues, then they can march on into failure. Jesus redeemed what appeared to be failure and used it as foundational preparation. This is the "covenant of Sure Mercy" in action.

Matthew 23 records the fruit of refusing the preparational process that God ordains. Verses 23–25 state:

> *Woe to you, scribes and Pharisees, hypocrites. For you pay tithe of mint and anise and cummin, and have neglected the weightier matters of the law: justice and mercy and faith. These you ought to have done, without leaving the others undone. Blind guides, who strain out a gnat and swallow a camel. Woe to you, scribes and Pharisees, hypocrites. For you cleanse the **outside** of the cup and dish, but **inside** they are full of extortion and self-indulgence.*

The stated reason they came into judgment was that they made sure everything was perfect on the outside but refused to deal with heart issues. This could easily be a picture of our "most successful" churches. As pastors, if we never confront sin for fear of offending, we get a congregation just described. Jesus never wavered in confronting sin. Some pastors build their churches by avoiding it. Let me ask you, do you think giving into an altar that is silent on important scriptures causes multiplication in your finances? I can guarantee you it won't. "Blind Pharisee, first cleanse the **inside** of the cup and dish, that the **outside** of them may be clean also." Where does purity start? Purity starts at an altar that preaches the whole counsel of God's Word, not just part of it.

Preaching only the blessing is "gospel lite" that may well produce an eternal weight so heavy its participants end up in the wrong place, depending on heart motivation!

Verse 29–33 of Matthew 23 says:

> *Woe to you, scribes and Pharisees, hypocrites. Because you build the tombs of the prophets and adorn the monuments of the righteous, and say, "If we had lived in the days of our fathers, we would not have been partakers with them in the blood of the prophets." Therefore you are witnesses against yourselves that you are sons of those who murdered the prophets. Fill up, then, the measure of your fathers' guilt. Serpents, brood of vipers. How can you escape the condemnation of hell?*

What was the judgment that came to the generation that refused to let Jesus do heart surgery? They lost their anointing first, and then they lost their positional authority. And they lost it in that order. And we are going to see those same things again. It is coming. So **what is the chief issue right now?** The issue is, what is the condition of our hearts?

Jesus began speaking to these issues very early in the Sermon on the Mount when He said, "Therefore if we bring our gift to the altar. . . ." THIS IS VERY EXPLICIT. Matthew calls each individual to account over their heart condition before addressing the corporate condition of the altar which reflects the Priest's heart condition. Matthew 23 specifically addresses how the leadership is conducting the corporate altar. Matthew 5, on the other hand, reveals the individual's responsibility before approaching the altar to consummate covenant. We would be wise to judge ourselves before we attempt to judge others. "Therefore if you bring your gift to the altar, and there remember that your brother has something against you, leave your gift there before the altar, and go your way." "If we feel like it" is not a given option. "When it is convenient" is not a possibility. "If we could just connect with the person on the phone" is not part of the passage. There is a terrible word right in the middle of verse 24. It has horrible consequences. It is the word, "**first**" not second, tenth or twenty-ninth. "**First** be reconciled to your brother, and then come and offer your gift." The covenant promises for blessing are awesome. The covenant responsibilities of qualifying are not negotiable. We cannot expect the covenant to work unless we are willing to get our relationships straight. This passage offers a blinking neon spiritual light. Stop. Straighten out broken relationships, *and then* give the gift. Only then will our gift be sanctified and the covenant consummated. Do we have a string of broken relationships? Woe is us. We must change our behavior and grow in relationship.

Here is the inescapable conclusion. Broken relationships bring our own impurity to the altar hindering covenantal blessing. Traumatic experiences at an early age can become an underground root sending branches to the surface reproducing the pain. God is quite faithful to reveal actions and attitudes which come from past experiences. He brings us into seasons where the roots keep surfacing demanding corresponding action. God ordains seasons of spiritual heart surgery. In such a season, my recommendation is to jump on the gurney and call for the anesthesiologist. And what will the fruit of this surgery be? Hopefully, the fruit will include setting an example for the next generation, opening the windows of heaven, and knowing in our hearts if we do our job right, we are not only going to change church structure and government, but we are going to build a platform for the next generation. They will not have to fight the battle of re-establishing integrity of leadership because we will have completed the task. They will not be hindered by finances but wholly given to the harvest.

God brings us to seasons
Where our roots must go deep,
And our hearts be made pure
His anointing to keep.

Sign up for heart surgery
And flow in God's best,
Jump up on the gurney
Put God to the test

CHAPTER 13

"POWER OF OFFENSES"

Romans 12:1 says, "I beseech you therefore, brethren, by the mercies of God, that you present your bodies a living sacrifice, holy, acceptable to God, which is your reasonable service." Psalm 118:27 is the verse which could easily follow Romans 12:1, "God is the LORD, And He has given us light; Bind the sacrifice with cords to the horns of the altar." The reason we have to **bind** is the same reason Abram bound his son. When the sacrifice is **living** and the fire falls, the tendency is to jump off the altar and run away. There is a promise that God gives if we stay on the altar until the fire has completed its work. It is a great one. It is a promise we can hear in our spirit. "**Well done**, good and faithful servant." I often think the biggest problem we have in five-fold ministry is we have too many rare and medium-rare leaders. God is strictly looking for the well-done crowd.

Matthew 5:20 says, "For I say to you, that unless your righteousness exceeds the righteousness of the scribes and Pharisees, you will by no means enter the kingdom of heaven." Kingdom authority awaits those who pass spiritual tests. What will we do when the Lord presents us with a spiritual bridge leading into Kingdom authority but it costs our media ministry? Will we run across the bridge? Will we jettison star status for authority that frees the church? Is there a price to manifesting the Kingdom? Does the Kingdom of heaven have anything to do with heaven or is it used for God's rule and reign here? Matthew 19:23–24 state:

> *Then Jesus said to His disciples, "Assuredly, I say to you that it is hard for a rich man to enter the kingdom of heaven. And again I say to you, it is easier for a camel to go through the eye of a needle than for a rich man to enter the kingdom of God.*

"Kingdom of heaven" and "kingdom of God" are often used interchangeably in the New Testament. The context of Matthew 19 is the struggle of the Rich Young Ruler with the spirit of mammon. He cannot quite cross the spiritual bridge. Verse 22 says, "But when the young man heard that saying, he went away sorrowful, for he had great possessions." What will we do if our bridge is relational? Will we wind up in the same sorrowful place? In Hebrews 11, faith is the fruit of obedience when God witnesses to us that we have pleased Him. The issue in view is governmental authority, not eternity. This passage is not necessarily talking about eternal life. It addresses the rule and reign of God right here and now in the earth. We are talking about the power to change circumstances. The goal is God's covenant promises manifesting in our behalf as we pursue an endtime harvest.

Matthew 5:21–22 say:

> *You have heard that it was said to those of old, "You shall not murder," and whoever murders will be in danger of the judgment. But I say to you that whoever is angry with his brother without a cause shall be in danger of the judgment. And whoever says to his brother, "Raca!" shall be in danger of*

the council. But whoever says, "You fool!" shall be in danger of hell fire.

Verse 22 is a message all by itself. Three different levels of judgment are presented from all sides of an issue. One side addresses causing offense. The other side confronts the frustration of strained relationships where issues like anger must be addressed.

Verse 23 emphasizes our actions: "Therefore if you bring your gift to the altar, and there remember that your brother has something against you. . . ." Where verse 22 deals with frustration and anger over *somebody else's* behavior, verse 23 focuses on our actions or reactions having a very hindering impact. We are held accountable for our responses. We cannot change how others act and react, but we can change our own responses to them. Matthew 5:23–24 warns about the impact of our actions whether intended or not. We are responsible for straightening out misperceptions when made aware. God declares war on strife and demands we address it for our own benefit. ". . . Leave your gift there before the altar, and go your way. First be reconciled . . ." is radical. From this passage, we realize that relationships potentially impact the purity of an altar as much as proper use of tithe and offering. Jesus warned us not to complete our covenant of giving if our relationships were out of harmony. The message is to stop what we are doing and resolve the strife before completing the covenant.

Strained relationships with each other nullify covenant promises. How can we blame the altar where we sow for no provision if our personal relationships are fractured? How can God bless the relationship of giving with financial provision if personal relationships are never restored? This principle emanates from the ultimate Fatherhood of God. God is a Father who makes relational demands on His kids. A certain laying down of soul-life is expected. We act in the church as if we can selectively choose.

Jesus lived the opposite pattern. We live as if we have the right to selectively choose whether to deal with relationship issues by resolution or separation. We usually choose separation by finding another fellowship. This is today's Christian standard operating procedure. It permeates the church.

Today's cultural Christianity refuses the cross of obedience by following the path of least resistance. Is it any wonder we do not have the windows of heaven open? We love the covenant blessing, but the more we learn about what God wants from us to qualify, the more we begin to think, "Oh, no!" Walking in the covenant demands big change. We have not accepted the Word until we do the Word. How can we demand His covenant provision for end-time promises like the "Anointing to Spoil" if we refuse to obey simple relational guidelines? The answer is—we can't. Jesus does not demand we satisfy the objections of the world but covenant relationships within the believing community.

God demands we cultivate harmony in covenant relationships. That means when offenses come, whether through us or to us, the requirement is we get nose-to-nose and work it out. Christlikeness develops in hard places. When God wants to deal with our hearts, the pressure is usually to move or retreat. The Holy Spirit knows when we need to stay and when it is time to move. We should require at least one burning bush before we consider leaving a church. By running when things get tough, we usually thwart God's growth and development. Very few in the church actually obey the Matthew 18 resolution pattern. Step one in resolution is we must meet and talk with the offending individual. At such a meeting, we lovingly explain how their actions made us feel. Speaking the truth in love is a vital key. I believe ninety-five percent of all offenses could be settled at this level if we would simply **do** God's Word. Good books have been written to help the church in this process. One of the best I have ever read is *Caring Enough to Confront*. The author presents five different methods of confrontation and shows how Jesus used each one of them. It gives us the nuts and bolts of "how-to" sit down and work things out. Most of us develop a pattern of implementation or avoidance at home. Doing the Word begins at home.

How do we deal with anger and the incarcerating issue of the power of an offense? Matthew 5:25–26 state:

> *Agree with your adversary quickly, while you are on the way with him, lest your adversary deliver you to the judge, the judge hand you over to the officer, and you are thrown into prison. Assuredly, I say to you, you will by no means get out of there till you have paid the last penny.*

The context is between believers. **Jesus is talking about captivity resulting from an offense that we cause.** Jesus made us responsible for the offenses we cause.

Refusing to address offenses we cause can have a dramatic financial impact. **We do not see the altar of giving as a place of judgment, but God does.** If we consistently give without seeing fruit, we could easily question the purity of the altar. Once the gift of suspicion has been activated, "the accuser of the brethren" follows. We can fault others while overlooking the root issue—our behavior. Where are our hearts concerning resolving broken relationships? Have we offended anyone recently? Many of us experience a season of grace where God winks at our brokenness in the area of relationships. But eventually in the march toward maturity, the season ends and responsibility comes home to roost!

Scripture points us to covenant relationship where we learn to speak the truth in love. All marriages demand conflict resolution and learning to live in covenant. Church life is no different. We think it is different because we do not allow God to rule over us. Every leader who embraces the seeker-sensitive approach eventually has to face the unintended consequences of contributing to the lack of God's rule. We think we can go anywhere we like and anywhere that feels good. These factors contribute to the American churches' impotence in the face of the onslaught of Islam, abortion and sodomite marriage. Jesus reminds us the church is supposed to be the salt of the earth, but when salt loses its saltiness, it is good for nothing. As all barriers against perversion are removed and fullness of iniquity abounds, who will Jesus hold accountable for the loss of ability to defend our land? When the church forfeits its salt, devastation looms.

Why is Jesus so specific about addressing conflict? I believe one of the reasons is because of the power of agreement. Consequently, when we refuse to deal with offenses, the enemy of our soul has stolen one of our greatest God-appointed assets. The root issue here is which city do we want to build? God's city has to be built God's way, but mystery Babylon of Revelation represents building God's city *man's* way. Trying to build God's city (Kingdom) *man's* way is very popular, because there is **no cross** in it and little personal sacrifice.

Spiritual Babylon has definite characteristics and is not to be confused with a physical place in Iraq. There seems to be an abundance of evidence to convict some leaders in the American church of building it right here. To find the prime characteristics of the spirit of Babylon, all we have to do is run our Greek Concordance references on the root word for merchandising, **em-por-ee-on,** out of John 2 where Jesus first overturns the tables of the moneychangers and says, "Make not My Father's house a house of merchandise!" **Empor-ee-on** means, in context, to turn something holy into a merchandise mart and profit from it. The whole chapter of Revelation 18 deals with spiritual Babylon merchandising the gospel and its impact on nations. How can we biblically define a "merchandise mart" where "selling" the gospel becomes paramount? Putting a price on material does not qualify as a "merchandise mart" because of 1 Corinthians 9:12–14:

> *If others are partakers of this right over you, are we not even more? Nevertheless we have not used this right, but endure all things lest we hinder the gospel of Christ. Do you not know that those who minister the holy things eat of the things of the temple, and those who serve at the altar partake of the offerings of the altar? Even so the Lord has commanded that those who preach the gospel should live from the gospel.*

This passage authorizes ministers to reasonably live from what they produce. Building an **em-por-ee-on** (merchandise mart) or using the **kap-ale-yoo-o** (peddling) tactics moves us into disqualifying territory!

Genesis 11 reveals the foundational motivational root necessary to build our own city. Genesis 11:1–4 states:

> *Now the whole earth had one language and one speech. And it came to pass, as they journeyed from the east, that they found a plain in the land of Shinar, and they dwelt there. Then they said to one another, "Come, let us make bricks and bake them thoroughly." They had brick for stone, and they had asphalt for mortar. And they said, "Come, let us build **ourselves** a city, and a tower whose top is in the heavens; let us make a **name for ourselves**, lest we be scattered abroad over the face of the whole earth."*

Now we have a comparison of two cities. The city Abraham was looking for described in Hebrews 11 was quite different. Its builder and maker was God. Two different cities are being built: God's (New Jerusalem) and man's (Babylon). To which one are we contributing? What is the difference between the two cities? One major difference is in the foundation. One has foundations whose builder and maker is God. The other has foundations based on self, what feels and looks good, is desirable to the eyes and makes one wise—its called Babylon. The difference is in the spirit of the founder. Who founded Babylon? The answer is in Genesis 10:8:

> *"Cush begot Nimrod; he began to be a mighty one on the earth. He was a mighty hunter before the LORD; therefore it is said, 'Like Nimrod the mighty hunter before the LORD.' And the beginning of his kingdom was Babel . . ."* [i.e. Babylon].

What was his motivation? Genesis 11:4 tells, "And they said, 'Come let us build ourselves a city, and a tower whose top is in the heavens. . . .'" Josephus says the motivation was to build it above the level of God's judgment which they had experienced in the flood. They wanted to build a system that was above or beyond the judgment of God. How do we do that in the earth today? The chief ingredient is financial success. We must make it palatable enough for a successful sale. If we can sell it, and if we do it in the right way, we insulate ourselves against adversity. Jesus said, "Freely you have received, freely give." We insulate ourselves against the harness of God, enabling us to do whatever we want, which is the essence of Babylon. We do not have to completely depend on God if there is a way we can do it *ourselves*. But what does that require? In order to be profitable with whatever media we choose, we have to make a name for ourselves. Marketing is the key: ". . . Let us make a name for **ourselves**. . . ." How much Babylon are we building? Are we making "men of God" or "men of Gold"? Would it be a shock to find mystery Babylon of Revelation 18 operating among us daily? Revelation 18:2 says:

> *And he cried mightily with a loud voice, saying, "Babylon the great is fallen, is fallen, and has become a habitation of*

demons, a prison for every foul spirit, and a cage for every unclean and hated bird. For all the nations have drunk of the wine of the wrath of her fornication, the kings of the earth have committed fornication with her, and the merchants of the earth have become rich through the abundance of her luxury."

Verse 11 decrees:

*And the **merchants** of the earth will weep and mourn over her, for no one buys their **merchandise** anymore.*

Verses 15–16 declare:

*The **merchants** of these things, who became rich by her, will stand at a distance for fear of her torment, weeping and wailing, and saying 'Alas, alas, that great city that was clothed in fine linen, purple, and scarlet, and adorned with gold and precious stones and pearls!*

Verse 20 says:

Rejoice over her, O heaven, and you holy apostles and prophets, for God has avenged you on her.

Ask yourself what spirit determined to destroy Jesus immediately after His second and final cleansing of the Temple. When Jesus cleansed the Temple at the beginning of His ministry in John 2, He stopped the "merchandising" (**em-por-ee-on**). Merchandising is what merchants (**em-poros**) do. But when mammon is involved, it becomes a major avenue of defilement. Men will do anything to protect their "cash cow." Verses 23 and 24 describe this spirit, "And the light of a lamp shall not shine in you anymore." It did at one time. They had light at one time and lost it.

*. . . And the voice of bridegroom and bride shall not be heard in you anymore. For your **merchants** were the great men of the earth, for by your sorcery all the nations were deceived. And in her was found the blood of prophets and saints, and of all who were slain on the earth.*

What is the consistent thing that mystery Babylon exudes? Satan's use of mammon counterfeits the work of the Holy Spirit in the life of a believer. Mystery Babylon spews and infects everything it touches with one message: Do whatever necessary to be a success. Jesus was so successful representing the Father that they killed Him. Which is more successful today: 1) building a megachurch (one percent of the population of your city) or 2) being martyred? This raises the question of when is church CHURCH? For those who continually package and promote, the issue here is motivation of heart, not price on product.

When the spirit of Babylon is confronted, it only knows one response: destroy the threat in any way possible. Mammon motivates, manufactures and markets for money while the Holy Spirit motivates, manufactures and markets for Kingdom growth. Mammon is like the AIDS virus—once infected, it is nearly impossible to cure and nearly always leads to death. Genesis 11:5–6 says, "But the LORD came down to see the city and the tower which the sons of men had built." This city had a foundation built on rebellion. "And the LORD said, 'Indeed the people are one and they all have one language, and this is what they begin to do; now nothing they propose to do will be withheld from them.'"

If emerging apostolic and prophetic ministries adopt the fundraising principles of the last generation, the whole move will end in judgment. What spirit permeates this stream of Christianity? Who do we worship if we gain members by refusing to preach certain passages? Revelation 18:20 says, "Rejoice over her, O heaven, and you holy apostles and prophets, for *God has* avenged you on her!" Mammon permeates our religious system and continually reveals itself when challenged. Why is apostolic team ministry a potential threat to the spirit of mammon? God is using restoration to reveal hearts. A religious system that is mammon-based will see any new thing as a threat structurally. Big threats demand big assaults. Releasing people to obey the Holy Spirit shouldn't be a threat. But when we do it in the area of giving, if a system is mammon-based, we have war. Where in the Bible does anyone sell covering and oversight for ten percent, or five percent, or three percent a month? How about demanding the organization be placed on every church bank account, enabling seizure of funds at will? Peter would have pronounced Ananias and Sapphira judgments on anyone who suggested it. You can see the repercussions of what we are talking about. You can imagine how popular this message is. "The Cost of Buying and Selling the Gospel" is the simple issue of: Are we building God's Kingdom or setting up mystery Babylon? The two are mutually exclusive. We are either doing one or the other. Which one is it? Just a hint or sniff of motivational mammon means we are building Babylon denominationally or independently. Sniff, sniff, sniff!

Genesis 11:6 and 7 say:

And the LORD said, "Indeed the people are one and they all have one language, and this is what they begin to do; now nothing that they propose to do will be withheld from them. Come, Let Us go down and there confuse their language, that they may not understand one another's speech."

What was such a threat? They were in agreement. They had the same vision. They were in harmony. And God said, ". . . nothing they propose to do will be withheld from them." What does that tell us about the power of agreement? The Old Testament word for the fruit of agreement is **shalom**. It means peace, prosperity, blessing and divine provision It covers the whole spectrum. In the New Testament, there is a Greek word that corresponds to **shalom** and it is called **i-ray-nay**. Jesus is called the Prince of **I-ray-nay**/Peace. What is the fruit of harmony and agreement? It is peace. ". . . Can two walk together unless they be agreed?" No. What is the fruit of getting in harmony with God? It is peace. When many in the church world seem to be hurriedly going south, there is a "knowing" planted in our hearts; even though we are paddling upstream, we know we are going to make it.

What would we do if the food distribution system was suddenly interrupted? Having grown up on a farm, I have thought of this more than once in the last few years. If food distribution breaks down, some of our major cities would see supermarket wars. We could see gang wars over food. Most people do not know how to put food on the table from the land. We are totally dependent on Kroger, Safeway, Price Club and Wal-Mart. Growing up on a farm is a lost experience. While growing up, I learned how to live off the land. It was much harder than going to a store. The majority of America could not live off the land. We know how to find McDonald's. Franchising in the church is a lot like the food distribution system. How long will the church provide Happy Meals? Jesus was consistently led to confront sin and speak truth which left His listeners anything but happy!

Most people do not know anything different because we have been doing it the same way for years. Did "fast food" beget "fast church"? Where is the beef? What is the fruit? Is our nation more or less godly? When are we fed up enough to make changes?

How can we grow our faith to walk in a different way? The answer is in Hebrews 11, and it is called a **mar-too-reh-o** witness. **Mar-toos** is the Greek word for the witness you and I give. Acts 1:8 says, "But you shall receive power when the Holy Spirit has come upon you; and you shall be witnesses to Me in Jerusalem, and in all Judea and Samaria, and to the end of the earth." **Martoos** is the word from which we get martyr. But **mar-too-reh-o** is the other side of the coin. It is the witness God gives to us when we obey Him. When we choose to do His Word, we are in harmony with His will, and in agreement with Him. Our action releases a response. He drops something in our hearts. Now what will that produce? The first fruit it produces is faith. Only God can give it. We cannot get it anywhere else. In the Bible, this witness produced a faith that escaped death. Enoch got a witness and escaped death. How do we get God to give us such a witness? It usually comes when we choose to use our faith on our flesh to obey Him. First John says, "Don't say you love Me when you see a brother in need" and pass on by. In other words, He says that our agreement in walking with Him is demonstrated in how we deal with each other. If we want the power of the covenant promises without paying the price in relationships, we are deluded. God demands we love each other not in word but in deed.

The Power of Agreement

Matthew 18:19 is a great New Testament promise based on the power of agreement, "Again I say to you that if two of you agree on earth concerning anything that they ask, it will be done for them by My Father in heaven." But what is the context? The context is restoring somebody who is offending people. God demands we deal with offenses to maintain the seedbed of our relational covenant within the church.

Colossians 3:15 says that the fruit of agreement will lead us to make decisions that reflect God's perfect will. In *The Amplified Bible* it says, "Let the peace of God rule and settle with finality all thoughts and questions in your mind. Let it act as an umpire over every decision you make." There is no lasting peace outside of relationship with God and He demands we get in right relationship with each other. The opposite of peace is strife, which comes from the Greek word **er-ith-i-ah**, meaning electioneering for office, self-advancement, or a hireling. I always wondered what defined the John 10 hireling. The root word **er-is** means wrangling or contention manifested through a divisive spirit.

James 3:13–18 states:

> *Who is wise and understanding among you? Let him show by good conduct that his works are done in the meekness of wisdom. But if you have bitter envy and self-seeking [strife] in your hearts, do not boast and lie against the truth. This wisdom does not descend from above, but is earthly, sensual, demonic. For where envy and self-seeking [strife] exist, confusion and every evil thing will be there. But the wisdom that is from above is first pure, then peaceable, gentle, willing to yield, full of mercy and good fruits, without partiality and without hypocrisy. Now the fruit of righteousness is sown in peace by those who make peace.*

If we come to the altar to do business with God while permitting **er-ith-i-ah** in our heart, we are hurting ourselves. It is a prison house experience. Mark 9:33 says:

> *Then He came to Capernaum. And when He was in the house He asked them, "What was it you disputed among yourselves on the road?" But they kept silent, for on the road they had disputed among themselves who would be the greatest.*

Jesus chose disciples full of self-seeking—**er-ith-i-ah**—in action. Only an application of the cross can redeem us from self-seeking. If the cross is seldom preached, then self-seeking resides in many personal altars. At the height of convention center meetings, a mentality was spawned by many whose vision of successful ministry was simply to fill a convention center. God moved dramatically in convention centers, but His heart has always been in the local church. A strong component of asking to fill a convention center came from **er-ith-i-ah**.

God promises more anointing in winding up the age than was released to the early church who started it. He chose them with their flaws, just like He has chosen us with ours. Flaws, failures, spots, wrinkles and blemishes have never stopped God from calling people to be His children and work for Him. Once in the Kingdom, our obligation is to pursue Christlikeness, which means embracing servanthood and crucifying self-seeking. From the time He called the Twelve, to the night He went to Gethsemane, the same problem persisted.

Mark 9:34–37a says:

So they kept silent, for on the road they had disputed among themselves who would be the greatest. And He sat down, called the twelve, and said to them, "If anyone desires to be first, he shall be last of all and servant of all." Then He took a little child and set him in the midst of them. And when He had taken him in His arms, He said to them, "Whoever receives one of these little children in My name receives Me. . . ."

Why is it Jesus suddenly switches gears? He has been addressing the issue of strife, when suddenly He starts talking about receiving from others. He takes a little kid, sets him in the midst of the group and says, ". . . and whoever receives Me, receives not Me but Him who sent Me."

Verse 38 says, "Now John answered Him, saying, 'Teacher, we saw someone who does not follow us casting out demons in

Your name, and we forbade him. . . .'" **Ko-loo-o** is a pruning term. It means to take the shears and lop it off, totally severing it from the vine. ". . . And we cut him off because he does not follow us." Exclusivity comes from self-seeking and builds strife. Foundational motivation was bringing impurity to the altar through poisoning personal relationships. Harmony was destroyed among the Twelve and discernment fled. They could not recognize the betraying culprit. Once blinded, they were captive to unfolding events.

If we wonder why there are whole denominations or individual churches that will not receive what God is doing, look in this spiritual arena. God seems to be forming His own governmental structure. There are leaders who are absolutely scared to death of this emerging ministry model, probably because it is not based on a controllable commodity-mammon (five percent or ten percent a month).

Beware when ministry cannot discern what God is doing or why. Self-seeking destroyed their harmony by releasing strife and separating them from the wisdom of God. They could not discern the perpetrating party in their midst. Who speaks for God and who does not? This principle has not changed. It is still the same. And if there was ever a season that we need to get our relationships straight, it is right now.

There are two major pluses that are going to come about when we get into harmony. Plus #1 is the opening of spiritual eyes to discern the plans of the enemy. We begin to recognize his agents. Plus #2 is we begin to discern the voice of God even when it comes from unlikely candidates. Political positioning is being replaced with relationship. What kind of relationships do we have? The church is a family. The Twelve ministered together city by city and place to place. Occasionally, Jesus sent them out two-by-two. But most of the time they were together as a family.

Exclusivity developed probably from transfiguration-type experiences, and they made potentially disqualifying assumptions. Jesus said in verses 39–42 of Mark 9:

> *Do not forbid him, for no one who works a miracle in My name can soon afterward speak evil of Me. For he who is not against us is on our side. For whoever gives you a cup of water to drink in My name, because you belong to Christ, assuredly, I say to you, he will by no means lose his reward. And whoever causes one of these little ones who believe in Me to stumble, it would be better for him if a millstone were hung around his neck, and he were thrown into the sea.*

Who was Jesus addressing? Was John, the apostle of love, responding like a Mafia hit-man whose region had just been invaded? That gives me hope that some of the most obnoxious, offensive people in God's kingdom can be transformed. Something transpired here that went into the heart of John, grabbed him by the spiritual throat and turned him around. What was it? Jesus began to describe vividly and in detail the eternal fruit he would give account for if he did not straighten up and fly right and get a real change of heart. Jesus hammered the Twelve and then He said, "And if your hand makes you sin, cut it off." John had just "cut off" another believer and may have offended him. John, and the others agreeing with him, must have envisioned the millstone being placed around their necks dragging them quickly to the bottom. Verses 43–44 state:

> *. . . If your hand makes you sin, cut it off. It is better for you to enter into life maimed, than having two hands, to go to hell, into the fire that shall never be quenched—where "their worm does not die and the fire is not quenched."*

Jesus punctuated this warning by adding the same prohibition with the foot and the eye. Jesus was a hellfire and brimstone preacher. When needed, Jesus refused to soft-soap the truth. Are we speaking truth?

The hand speaks of what we "do" for God. What we "do" is hindered and we can never fulfill the call if our relationships are continually in disharmony. Our foot speaks of where God has called us to "go." The cities and the nations where we can have an impact are diminished unless we determine to get our relationships straight. God is first and foremost a Creator Who created us for relationship. The third arena is the eye, or the things God has called us to "see" in the realm of the spirit. What revelation will we forfeit if we neglect relationships? The Twelve are a perfect example. Jesus told them about God's timeline but they could not see it. There was betrayal in their midst. They could not see it. There was a man, not of their group, doing miracles that came across their path, but they saw it as a threat instead of a blessing. What we "do," where we "go," and what we "see" are dependent on keeping relationships free of strife, criticism, rancor and hostility. Being quick to repent when we miss it keeps the personal altar pure and the heavenly pipeline open!

Verse 49 says, "For everyone will be seasoned with fire, and every sacrifice will be seasoned with salt." Leviticus 2:13 is the foundational verse, "And every offering of your grain offering you shall season with salt; you shall not allow the salt of the covenant of your God to be lacking from your grain offering. With all your offerings you shall offer salt."

Numbers 18 tells us the origin of the tithe and offering when God gave it to the Levites. Numbers 18:19–20 states:

> *All the heave offerings of the holy things, which the children of Israel offer to the LORD, I have given to you and your*

*sons and daughters with you as an ordinance forever; it is a **covenant of salt** forever before the LORD with you and your descendants with you. Then the LORD said to Aaron: "You shall have no inheritance in their land, nor shall you have any portion among them; I am your portion and your inheritance among the children of Israel. . . ."*

Mark 9:49 says, "For everyone will be seasoned with fire, and every sacrifice will be seasoned with salt. Salt is good, but if the salt loses its flavor. . . ." This refers to the priestly function of salting and completing the covenant for the giver. How do we lose our ability to salt or sanctify the sacrifice, or complete the covenant? That is what the salt did. Salt was the sign of the covenant. When the priest added salt and spoke the blessing on the people, it completed the covenant. Jesus was warning the Twelve about losing the ability to speak the blessing on the covenant people. "Salt is good, but if the salt loses its flavor how will you season it? Have salt in yourselves. . . ." How do we do that? He tells us ". . . have peace with one another." The Greek word is **i-ray-nay**. No relational peace—no salt. No peace—no recognition. No peace—no discerning. No peace—no witness about God's will in a situation. How can I discern God's will? Where you find peace, you usually find God's wisdom.

Second Chronicles 28 and 29 prophetically describe a transition which would greatly benefit the church. Second Chronicles 28 characterizes an extended season of moral decline with intervening signposts alerting a potential disaster. Many nations have endured just such a season where they have seen adversity because of disobedience, moral relativism and religious indifference.

Second Chronicles 28:1 states:

Ahaz was twenty years old when he became king, and he

reigned sixteen years in Jerusalem; and he did not do what was right in the sight of the LORD, as his father David had done. For he walked in the ways of the kings of Israel, and made molded images for the Baals.

Verse 5 says, "Therefore the LORD his God delivered him into the hand of the king of Syria." When a nation's founders covenant with God, like America's did, then God deals unfavorably with the nation when they backslide or deny Him. When senators and representatives defy God, the nation groans under the adversity that these leaders engender. New milestones in judgment are achieved, such as becoming the greatest debtor nation in the history of the world. As perverse judges get approved, the righteous foundations of our forefathers are removed, championing defiling issues such as the shedding of innocent blood and homosexual marriage, crying out for judgment.

After thirty plus years of abortion on demand, we are over 50 million short of the population we should have. This deficit carries devastating judgments such as not enough workers paying money into Social Security to fund the retirees who are withdrawing money from it.

The population vacuum has helped create an illegal immigration nightmare that is making our borders uncontrollable and filling our land with a different culture. The severity of God is seen in the devastation of nations who continually spit in His face and refuse to repent. Why do we have this economic nightmare and mess? When our nation **turned from** God and embraced secularism, the judgments began. The knowing rejection of the Lord Jesus is bringing continual and ever-increasing devastations upon the land.

When we neglect relationships
Our impact is diminished,
Christ's words "WELL DONE"
We may not hear,
When finally our course is finished

Purifying the Altar

CHAPTER 14

DEVELOPING PEACE-FILLED RELATIONSHIPS

Second Chronicles 28:17 states:

> *For again the Edomites had come, attacked Judah, and carried away captives. The Philistines also had invaded the cities of the lowland and of the South of Judah, and had taken Beth Shemesh . . . and other cities.*

Verse 19 adds, "For the LORD brought Judah low because of Ahaz king of Israel, for he had encouraged moral decline in Judah and had been continually unfaithful to the LORD." Has America had leaders encouraging moral decline in the past half century? Do increasing numbers of politicians support abortion and homosexual marriage? Every time we vote for a senator or representative who supports abortion, homosexual marriage or civil unions (only semantical difference) we vote to fill the national cup of iniquity guaranteeing devastating judgments on the land.

What happened in Judah while Ahaz reigned is essentially what has occurred in Western society in the last fifty years. And what was the fruit of that? Captivity. The fruit of disobedience is always captivity. The church, like the prophets, must show an avenue of restoration. The covenant of "Sure Mercy" is such a place, but demands a foundation of practicing it with our own leaders who face moral failure. A good place to start might be with our relationships. Harmony is the foundation of Christian power. Strife is Satan's ploy to nullify that power. The time to deal with relationships is now. Maximizing harmony can prepare us to face seasons of adversity by insulating us from major devastation. Obedience now may well become our platform for speaking life in the near future. The anointing will be needed in a catastrophic hour.

Scripture promises a great harvest but we must be prepared. Part of being properly positioned is developing peaceful relationships. Minimizing offense is one aspect of this, but equally if not more important is "receiving correction and reproof." Having a teachable spirit is a necessary part to receiving correction and reproof, releasing peace. God's corrective process almost always comes with a dose of humility. And we have to choose to humble ourselves to receive. The process can usually be summed up as a crucifying experience. It may bring death to our flesh and to the pride of life, but the end result is wonderful. Who brought correction through captivity to Judah? Verse 19 says it was not the devil. The Bible says the LORD did it. Why? So Judah would turn to Him. If we can discern the spirit of Babylon operating in Ahaz, then possibly we can deal with it in our own nation!

Second Chronicles 28:24 says:

> *So Ahaz gathered the articles of the house of God, cut in pieces the articles of the house of God, shut up the doors of the house of the LORD, and made for **himself** altars in every corner of Jerusalem.*

"Let us make for **ourselves** a name. . . ." How long did Ahaz rule and reign? He led for only sixteen years. The fruit of disobedience was you died before your time. You never fully arrived at where God wanted you to go. You never saw all He ordained for you to see. You never did all He had assigned for you to do. We seem to have returned to the principle of the hand, foot and eye.

Verse 27 states:

> *So Ahaz rested with his fathers, and they buried him in the city, in Jerusalem; but they did not bring him into the tombs of the kings of Israel. Then Hezekiah his son reigned in his place.*

Chapter 29, verse 1, says:

> *Hezekiah became king when he was twenty-five years old, and he reigned twenty-nine years in Jerusalem. His mother's name was Abijah the daughter of Zechariah. And he did what was right in the sight of the LORD, according to all that his father David had done. In the first year of his reign, in the first month, he opened the doors of the house of the LORD and repaired them.*

Verses 4–5:

> *Then he brought in the priests and the Levites, and gathered them in the East Square, and said to them: 'Hear me,*

Levites. Now sanctify yourselves, sanctify the house of the LORD God of your fathers, and carry out the rubbish from the holy place. . . .'

But we cannot carry rubbish out of the holy place until God reveals His definition of rubbish. How much of what we do is rubbish to God? Effective ministry always dramatically increases when waves of renewal reveal God's purposes. This whole passage is a pertinent picture in type and shadow of what can happen when a generation says "yes" to God. The fruit of it is a victory and a blessing that the Scripture seems to indicate went way beyond Solomon's achievements.

I believe the church in the last days is going to participate in an outpouring that goes beyond anything any generation has seen or known. As demonic fullness reaches its apex, divine fullness must also be displayed through the church. Satan's activities will be putting a demand on the "fullness of God!"

One amazing element of this story is the very first thing Hezekiah does at his young age when assuming the throne. In the first month, he opens the doors to the house of the LORD. Prophetic revelation was planted at a young age. Hezekiah overcame the rebellion of his father to become a great and godly king.

What is the spiritual application of opening the doors to the house of the LORD and repairing them? I remember seasons where my doors of perception were closed over the issue of the cross. I was learning about faith, but my teachers discouraged the cross, closing doors which would cause great hurt. Some have closed their doors to the restoration of apostolic and prophetic ministry. Some churches have closed their doors to women in ministry. Most in the American church closed their doors to understanding a season of persecution. Opening spiritual doors is a major prophetic challenge. One blessing, which usually emerges from restoring relationships, is the opening of doors. We start seeing things we have never seen before. One spiritual law states when God shows you something, even though it may be for another generation, you can usually participate in it by faith.

God opened the revelational doors for David and he saw the day when all God's people would be priests. He was the only one in the Old Testament God permitted to operate as both a king and a priest. Obedience to the Holy Spirit usually opens revelational doors. The issue is, are we willing to pay the price to qualify? Sometimes that price means staying in a church where we would rather leave. Loving people in their offensive behavior can be a crucifixion. The season has come. It is here. The question is, how are we going to respond? What are we going to do with the challenge? If God leads us to stay in a church with an impure altar, it is our job to pray purity into manifestation.

If we were going to pray for the purification of our own altar, how would we pray?

Suggested Prayer

Lord, we come before Your throne right now as a people who need Your mercy and a people who need Your grace. O Lord God, giver of every good and perfect gift, open our doors. Open the doors of our hearts to deal with areas of our lives that we have locked up and refused to face. And whenever anybody got close or touched a painful memory, we went another way. We threw up our defenses and said we're not going to talk about that or else we just went to another church. Lord, open our doors. Give us an ear to hear from that individual who grates on our flesh and we can hardly stand. Give us an ear to hear what they have to say. Oh, Our Father, do a work that only you can do. Stretch out Your hand in our behalf and give us the grace to no longer hide from one another but to be honest, speaking the truth, opening our lives in fellowship and in sharing. Give us a heart to deal with offenses in the way you ordained, no longer to run from each other but toward each other with all our heart, might and being. Lord, we thank You for grace—we receive it. We ask You to bless us now to walk it out in the weeks and months ahead. Help us be the people that discern the doings of the enemy and the promptings of our God—a people thoroughly prepared and ready for a harvest accepting the move of Your Spirit. Lord, we thank You for it. We ask You to bring it forth. Now stretch out Your hand and accomplish it, in Jesus' Name.

How do you react
To reproof and correction,
When God uses others
To tweak your direction?

Do you respond humbly
When you are offended,
Then closer to God's heart
You have ascended.

One corner pillar
That prepares us for power,
Are brethren UNITED
HERE no thief can devour.

Lord, I welcome Your dealings
In my heart today,
Give me ears that will listen
And a WILL to obey.

CHAPTER 15

"CULTIVATING REPROOF"

The covenant of the tithe offers both an awesome promise and a confrontational challenge. The awesome promise is opening the windows of heaven. The promise of Malachi 3 uses the same word as when God sent the flood of Noah. Opening the windows is no small deal. Not having room enough to receive it presents a concept far beyond the experience of most Christians. This is blessing a person to the point of embarrassment. Who can imagine apologizing for what God has done. If we purify the corporate altar to the point where it actually sanctifies and completes the covenant, then the chief area of concern becomes the individual condition of each offerer. A failure to love through offense can be really costly. If we are going to take the time to give, we might as well claim the covenantal return by fulfilling the requirements. Matthew 5:23–26 states:

> *Therefore if you bring your gift to the altar, and there re-*

member that your brother has something against you, leave your gift there before the altar, and go your way. First be reconciled to your brother, and then come and offer your gift. Agree with your adversary quickly, while you are on the way with him, lest your adversary deliver you to the judge, the judge hand you over to the officer, and you are thrown into prison. Assuredly, I say to you, you will by no means get out of there till you have paid the last penny.

Perhaps the first question to be asked for tithers is, "Are we experiencing financial prison?" How long is the duration of the financial drought and if it has prison parallels, then we should heed the biblical warnings of this passage.

The "kingdom of heaven" and "kingdom of God" are used interchangeably, meaning the Kingdom Jesus preached is as active now as when He preached it. The rule and reign of Christ is available. God's promises can be covenantally claimed. We cannot claim manifestations of covenant promises unless we live according to covenant commands. By accepting Jesus as Lord and Savior, we enter blood covenant. All He has bought and paid for belongs to us and all we have gained belongs to Him. Within the covenant family (church, home and hopefully nation), the demand is clear: we love each other as Jesus loved us. Broken relationships open the door for more than physical adversaries to steal from us. By entertaining unforgiveness and strife, over time, bitterness emerges in the atmosphere where every evil work is conceived.

Verse 23 makes the impact clear,

Therefore if you bring your gift to the altar, and there remember that your brother has something against you, leave your gift there before the altar. . . .

Why? Because the covenant promises are not going to work until we attempt to reconcile relationship. An honest attempt qualifies on our part even if it is rejected. In this aspect of purifying the altar, we begin to realize God put a demand on us that we learn to live in covenant with each other. The fruit of not learning this lesson is scattered throughout every church recorded in loss. The devil has used "divide and conquer" tactics. Count all the churches of the same denomination in small cities.

I will never forget the first night I spent in a city of ten thousand in West Texas. God woke me up at two a.m. in my motel room. This was a one-time event. I have never had this happen in any other city. He said, "Look in the Yellow Pages under 'Churches.'" So I did. And to my amazement I found three Nazarene churches, five Baptist churches, three Charismatic churches, two Pentecostal churches, two Methodist and one Catholic church. All main-line denominations were represented. I thought it was interesting that God would wake me up in the middle of the night to point that out, asking, "What spirit rules this city?" Disharmony and strife fostered by a **religious spirit** through "divide and conquer" had spiritually polarized people. Psalm 2 says to ask and God will give us cities and nations but we must qualify.

Matthew 5:24 says,

Leave your gift there before the altar, and go your way. First be reconciled to your brother, and then come and offer your gift. Agree with your adversary quickly. . . .

We do not often do that. Maybe we do not know how.

. . . While you are on the way with him, lest your adversary deliver you to the judge, the judge hand you over to the officer, and you are thrown into prison. Assuredly, I say to you, you will by no means get out of there. . . .

Are we experiencing captivity that never seems to end? Why haven't we been able to break out? Only satisfying the condition breaks the captivity. Jesus did some confrontation over relational issues with the disciples.

The Twelve learned this lesson the hard way. It is estimated that for at least two years Judas the betrayer had stolen from the moneybox without his peers discerning! How could you heal the sick, cast out devils and raise the dead for two years while daily rubbing shoulders with a thief and never see it? In another instance in Mark 9, they stopped a ministry from doing good work and had to be rebuked by Jesus. The disciples were as relationally challenged as most of us!

Mark 9:33–38 states:

> *Then He came to Capernaum. And when He was in the house He asked them, "What was it you disputed among yourselves on the road?" but they kept silent, for on the road they had disputed among themselves who would be the greatest. And He sat down, called the twelve, and said to them, "If anyone desires to be first, he shall be last of all and servant of all." Then He took a little child and set him in the midst of them. And when He had taken him in His arms, He said to them, "Whoever receives one of these little children in My name receives Me; and whoever receives Me, receives not Me but Him who sent Me." Now John answered Him, saying, "Teacher, we saw someone who does not follow us casting out demons in Your name and we forbade him (cut him off, stopped him in his tracks—there is an offense) because he does not follow us."*

What was the root of that behavior? Why did the future "apostle of love" act in such a possessive way? The man who became known for God's love did not start out that way. In Mark 10:35, James and John try to out-maneuver Peter by using their mother. The mother came to Jesus requesting, "That these two sons of mine can sit one on Your right hand and one on Your left?" When the other ten found out they were indignant. The selfish ambition of James and John to overtake Peter created strife. Strife is a seedbed for every evil work. It allows the enemy to hinder us. Strife can quench the gifts of the Spirit and close the door of provision. Jesus selected relationally dysfunctional misfits for ministry. Some things have not changed.

In Luke 22 Jesus noted in the Upper Room, "There is one who betrays Me at the table." As the Treasurer, Judas had been stealing from the till until mammon moved him to betray Jesus for thirty pieces of silver. This degenerate condition did not suddenly manifest but had a growth pattern previously documented. In addition to Judas, Jesus had to face the "Positional Competition" apparently generated by James, John and Peter. This was strong enough to have paralyzed any organization.

Relational captivity rendered them powerless to discern either light or darkness in their midst. The disciples had become blind in two dimensions. And what were the chief issues when the captivity of which Jesus warned were manifested? If we were the enemy, how would we stop the advance of God's Kingdom? Disagreement, division and strife through offense would accomplish this goal. And we wonder why we do not see things prophetically? Jesus emphasized the importance of relationships, and the necessity of keeping them straight. Mark 9:42 states, "And whoever causes one of these little ones who believe in Me to stumble. . . ." That Greek word is **skan-dal-id-zo**. Its root is **skan-dal-on**. It means to cause offense. ". . . It would be better for him if a millstone were hung around his neck, and he were thrown into the sea. And if your hand makes you sin, cut it off." To what was

Jesus referring? Who committed the sin Jesus was teaching about? What is the context? ". . . John answered Him, saying, 'Teacher, we saw someone who does not follow us casting out demons in Your name, and we shut down his ministry.'" The answer is Jesus' favorite disciple—John. This is one of the toughest rebukes Jesus delivered except for Peter's "Get behind Me, Satan" (Matthew 16:23).

The greatest corrections came to those who sought the highest leadership positions. Seeking position and favor can bring devastating personal correction. Those seeking great leadership position and great power should take note of how Jesus treated Peter (received the toughest rebuke, the failure of denying the Lord three times plus being sifted by Satan). This is what we can expect if we seek great power and position. The currency that spends best in the Kingdom is humility and servanthood. Having a millstone hung around our neck, and being thrown into the sea would not be pleasant. And if our hand makes us sin, cut it off. That is drastic action. **Ap-ok-op-to** means to amputate. Jesus is speaking figuratively. If we choose to disregard confronting offenses, then we walk around in a dimension of blindness. Neither can we discern what the enemy is doing, nor can we discern what God is doing.

The disciples arrived at such a place. That did not lessen God's commitment to them one bit. They were chosen. They were going to be used. Therefore, the Holy Spirit academy intensified their preparation. As they approached the end of Jesus' three and one-half years, a "no holds barred," "tell it like it is," "in your face Marine DI" approach was adopted.

> . . . *If your hand makes you sin, cut it off. It is better for you to enter into life maimed, than having two hands, to go to hell, into the fire that shall never be quenched.* . . .

"Cultivating Reproof"

We know Jesus never expected John was headed anywhere but heaven. He was speaking figuratively, but what an intense rebuke. Jesus was making a dramatic point, using natural things to spell out a spiritual truth. The spiritual truth was, if you do not let God deal with areas of your life and receive correction, you open the door for the loss of fruit that should be part of your eternal reward.

Works that God ordained before the foundations of the earth have to be protected. And Jesus uses three things which are symbolic to make His point. He uses "hand," "foot," and "eye." The **hand** signifies the works we are going to do, the **foot** speaks about the nations where God wants us to go, and the **eye** brings into view the things He wants us to see. Relational captivity can hinder growth at any one or all of these levels. If we are going to be fruitful and are ever going to come into the fullness of what God has for us, we must address relational issues. We have got to learn to live in covenant and that demands we learn to confront, giving and receiving reproof and correction. It is the one thing most believers do not want to do.

What did Jesus mean by, "Agree with your adversary quickly"? Agree means to resolve differences and symphonize. Are we willing to deal with offensive attitudes? Are we willing to deal with offensive traits? Are we willing to deal with offensive faults? **Skandal-id-zo** has a root which is **skan-dal-on**. It means a moveable stick or the trigger of a trap. The enemy pulls the trigger on the trap when he can get a predicted response. The enemy knows who is abrasive enough to push our buttons. Will we be trapped by **hand**, **foot** or **eye**? Have we walked into any bear traps lately? The root means to snare or to cause to stumble. **Skan-dal-id-zo** means to put an impediment in the way, to cause a person to distrust and desert the one he ought to trust and obey or receive from. How can the enemy cause us to distrust and desert Christian leaders we ought to trust and receive from? This scenario occurs weekly between the saints and leadership. When God gives leadership a directional word, the enemy is quick to point out a fault in their life, so we start magnifying the fault and we incarcerate ourselves in a place where we cannot receive needed direction from them. Many believers try to bring a ten-ton correction without paying the price to build a ten-ton bridge of relationship sustaining the weight of the correction.

In Mark 9, John was not just one of the Twelve; he was part of the inner circle. He went places Jesus did not take the other nine, like the Mount of Transfiguration. John saw the man doing deliverance as ministry competition, threatening his position of exclusivity. John had been captured by the pride of exclusivity. I wonder how many things we have in our lives, our personality, our attitudes, and our character traits that offend in both the church and world, while we are acting as Ambassadors for Christ. I remember sitting in the Dallas Airport waiting for a flight when I heard two men talking. One guy was talking about a friend at work who was a fanatical Christian. He was supporting an evangelist who had just been caught picking up a young girl for a sexual escapade. There I was listening to people in the world who were full of **skan-dal-id-zo** and **skan-dal-on** over church leaders. They were right next to me talking about it. Would you say they were prepared for a witness about Jesus? To see something in someone that causes them to distrust or disobey one they ought to trust and obey is an offense. The exhortation of Matthew 5 has one application to relationships hindering the growth of believers, but an entirely different weight when hindering salvation. We do not want to give an account for either.

"Cultivating Reproof"

Relational captivity
Must be replaced by unity,
It hinders growth and precious fruit
And does not end-time warriors suit.

Strife can quench the Spirit's gifts
As can vying for position,
Inviting every evil work
Closing doors of God's provision.

Have you been offensive
Or, maybe offended?
Are you caught in a feud
That has not yet been mended?

Is your unity spoiled
With an absence of fruit?
Are the storehouse doors open
For the devil to loot?

CHAPTER 16

THE PRICE OF GENERATING A WAVE!

Joel chapter 2:26–27 promises in two successive verses to remove all shame from the church. "And My people shall never be put to shame. . . . My people shall never be put to shame." Shame accumulates in seasons where covenant promises are significantly delayed. Waiting for God's perfect time can be a crucifixion of immense proportion. God's economy runs on a different standard and He reserves the right to spend our lives in ways not to our liking. The world honors those who accumulate, while God honors those who give. In the world, prestige is bestowed on those who accomplish, while God acknowledges those who attain Christlike character. Our culture promotes young rising stars, while God proves over time the faithfulness of His servants with adversity. The covenant promise is to pour out His glory and release an anointing that will eclipse all preparational shame. Parallel worlds functioning on different principles are everywhere in manifestation in our nation. The times and seasons of God traverse the generations allowing one generation years of character development and another hardly any.

I experienced a season where all I did was complain in prayer about the physical and financial adversity. God's answer to me was simple but profound. He said, "When you were born-again, filled with the Spirit and called to ministry in the Charismatic Renewal, you came into the middle of a movement that another generation paid to birth. It did not cost you anything. You came right in the middle. You caught the anointing. You surfed the wave. You saw the fruit of it." And I did, too. I saw the fruit of the gifts of the Spirit and their ability to alleviate pain and draw a crowd to build a ministry. Assembling a congregation was easy because of the flow of the Spirit. I caught it in a church that had built a prophetic seminary on the platform of an anointing so strong that people would drive through the parking lot and get healed. The gifts flowed like water. You could catch the flow and run with it. And many did.

Then the Lord said, "Now you have come to a season where it is your turn to pay the price to help birth a move of the Spirit." I call it the second and third generational plan. God promised Abram his seed would come out of captivity in the fourth generation. The job of the second and third generation was to sow the prophetic promises with such force and passion that the younger generation believed and prepared to walk in it. The major crucifixion is embracing and proclaiming what others will experience after you are gone. An unwanted transition is usually one where we pay the price while others get blessed. Generating a move of the Spirit and keeping it are two very different things. Every move of the Spirit since Azusa Street has been bled into oblivion by the same demonic progression. It starts with doctrinal debate degenerating into disagreement, division and ultimately the theological polarization that brings powerlessness.

Matthew 18:1–5 says, "At that time the disciples came to Jesus, saying, 'Who then is greatest in the kingdom of heaven?'" They had a disagreement, started to debate and division developed. They obviously still had not resolved their serious relational problems. Division has ministry-ending potential. Jesus declared the need for saved people to be converted in their thinking. The disciples' names were already written in heaven. Luke 10:20 says, ". . . Do not rejoice in this, that the spirits/devils are subject to you, but rather rejoice because your names are written in heaven." The needed "conversion" Jesus referred to (in Matthew 18) was not what we technically call "getting saved" or being "born-again." They were already believers.

The "conversion" identified was the process by which we move from flesh-dominated (whatever I want being paramount) to flesh-crucified (whatever God wants being paramount). Paul penned it in Galatians 4:19, "My little children, for whom I labor in birth again until Christ is formed in you." That is the "conversion" Jesus talked about. **Jesus was saying**, "Guys, look. Here is the way it is. Except *you be converted* and become as little children, you will by no means enter the authority, power and covenantal flow of God's Kingdom" (author's paraphrase). You have a royal invitation to participate in a Kingdom that is unseen until someone steps up in the anointing and authority to change what is seen. Blind eyes open, the lame walk, seeing eyes are made blind, corrupt and vile people hindering the harvest are incarcerated at your pronouncement. You become a walking plumbline. The choices you have made become the yardstick by which those around you are judged. Just walking into a church is enough to destroy it. Will we pay the preparational price?

Therefore, whoever humbles himself as "**this little child**. . . ."

How did that little child humble himself? Three distinct choices are of note. Number one, when Jesus called, he was ready because he chose to listen. He refused to so occupy and busy himself with personal things that he could not hear the Lord when He called. Many things clamor for our time. Carving out space for God is essential. How far ahead of where we are, would we be, if we implemented time to hear?

Matthew 18:4 states, "Therefore whoever humbles himself as this little child. . . ." How did the child humble himself? Number one, he chose to listen. Number two, when Jesus called he answered immediately, like Abraham with God's command to sacrifice Isaac.

Had we been Abraham, would we have pretended we did not hear it? Number three, he allowed Jesus to place him right where Jesus wanted him. Are we willing to conform our busy lives to God's purpose? Matthew 18:5–6 says:

> . . . *Whoever receives one little child like this in My name receives Me. But whoever causes one of these little ones who believe in Me to sin/stumble, it would be better for him if a millstone were hung around his neck.* . . .

Are we willing to kill a move of the Spirit because of offense or doctrinal hair-splitting? Matthew 18:7 sounds the same warning: "Woe to the world because of offenses. For offenses must come, but woe to that man by whom the offense comes. And if your hand or foot causes you to sin . . ." take drastic action. Christian maturity demands overcoming offenses. Verses 10 and 11 say, "Take heed that you do not despise one of these little ones, for I say to you that in heaven their angels always see the face of My Father who is in heaven. For the Son of Man has come to save that which was lost." Jesus was very clearly warning the Twelve about the impact of selfish ambition where their goals were born out of immaturity. They could easily cut themselves off from the covenant flow so their ministry was producing more damage than fruit, ultimately making God their enemy. Jesus went on to say in verses 12–15:

> *What do you think? If a man has a hundred sheep and one of them goes astray, does he not leave the ninety-nine and go to the mountains to seek the one that is straying? And if he should find it, assuredly, I say to you, he rejoices more over that sheep than over the ninety-nine that did not go astray. Even so it is not the will of your Father who is in heaven that one of these little ones should perish. Moreover if your brother sins against you, go and tell him his fault between you and him alone. If he hears you, you have gained your brother.*

Why don't we just simply do God's Word? The simple progression provides a 1-2-3-step process for resolving disputes where offense is involved. If we would embrace the process, we could keep our unity and possibly advance from faith-to-faith. The Lord gave the process. We have to accept it. How can we expect the windows of heaven to open if we are not willing to deal with our everyday relational issues? God promises something dramatic for the end-time church called the "Anointing to Spoil" but we cannot possess it if we do not purge the strife from our relationships.

God's times and His seasons
Are in His ordered plan,
Not set by the purpose
Of any mere man.

Are you careful to listen
When the Lord calls on you?
Do you respond quickly
When Christ wants you to?

Just as the small child
Will you give Him permission,
Toward directing your path
As a lifetime decision?

Then Christ's purpose you'll raise
Ushering in power and praise,
Perhaps the next wave
Won't be a brief phase.

CHAPTER 17

CULTIVATING CHARACTER THAT COUNTS

Jesus committed Himself to ultimate obedience. He chose to do what He saw and speak what He heard even unto death. Our marching orders are outlined in Matthew 10:24–27, which states:

> *A disciple is not above his teacher, nor a servant above his master. It is enough for a disciple that he be like his teacher, and a servant like his master. If they have called the master of the house Beelzebub, how much more will they call those of his household. Therefore do not fear them. For there is nothing covered that will not be revealed, and hidden that will not be known. Whatever I tell you in the dark, speak in the light; and what you hear in the ear, preach on the housetops.*

What was the final straw that got Jesus crucified? He exposed the impurity of the altar by addressing greed and manipulation. Reproof and correction are not popular. Developing the steel backbone to say what God wants said, even if people want to kill you for it, is the goal of spiritual growth for the prophetic. Jesus' chief resistance did not come from the world but the church. If we survive the church, we get to minister to the world. Jesus said that what He did we would do. To whom did Jesus send the Twelve initially? We are not talking about going first to the world. Verses 5–6 say:

> *These twelve Jesus sent out and commanded them, saying: "Do not go into the way of the Gentiles, and do not enter a city of the Samaritans. But go rather to the lost sheep of the house of Israel. . . ."*

The Twelve were sent to the church of their day. What can we expect when we speak the truth to the church? We are commanded to do it in love. What can we expect?

Verses 25–28 state:

> *It is enough for a disciple that he be like his teacher, and a servant like his master. If they have called the master of the house Beelzebub, how much more will they call those of his household. Therefore do not fear them. For there is nothing covered that will not be revealed, and hidden that will not be known. Whatever I tell you in the dark, speak in the light; and what you hear in the ear, preach on the housetops. And do not fear those who kill the body but cannot kill the soul. But rather fear Him who is able to destroy both soul and body in hell.*

Jesus demanded we speak what we hear even when it offends "religious" spirits. The war is on. How can an altar where a conscious ministry decision has been made to not confront sin ever sanctify any believer's giving? The Bible says Jesus is the same yesterday, today and forever, but the Jesus I hear about frequently bears little resemblance to the picture presented in Scripture.

Second Timothy 2:20–23 says:

> *But in a great house there are not only vessels of gold and silver, but also of wood and clay, some for honor and some for dishonor. Therefore if anyone cleanses himself from the latter, he will be a vessel for honor, sanctified and useful for the Master, prepared for every good work. Flee also youthful lusts; but pursue righteousness, faith, love, peace with those who call on the Lord out of a pure heart. But avoid foolish and ignorant disputes, knowing that they generate strife.*

What qualifies us to be a vessel of honor? Whenever we are confronted with a wrong attitude, or any reoccurring character issue and choose not to run from it, we choose the path of change or honor. If we run from it and hide, we become a vessel of dishonor. If we choose to deal with it, we become a vessel of honor. But what if there is never any confrontation from the pulpit so that a whole generation of believers are deprived of a biblical yardstick and cannot discern right from wrong? The greatest yardstick screaming this reality is how Christians vote. When a Christian votes for a candidate who supports homosexual rights and abortion, they demonstrate a scriptural ignorance so deep I seriously question if they were ever "born-again." When the discernment level is zero, the pastors are deceived and need to be replaced.

By supporting candidates who champion positions which

destroy the land, Christians will face judgment for making covenants with death and hindering the harvest. How can the simple and unsuspecting know unless leaders tell them? We have an obligation to teach truth. Therefore, when Christians vote, they need to know biblical right from biblical wrong. How can anyone who calls himself a Christian vote for a candidate who supports abortion? Don't we know that this fills a nation with iniquity inviting even more devastating judgments? Pastors do it all the time because they refuse to teach the truth for fear of losing people. We certainly do not teach a congregation to face issues by running from them as leaders. Do not waste your time putting money into a church that refuses to preach the whole unadulterated Word.

What is our habit in the church? Do we sit and face issues or run from them? Do we know people in various stages of deception? When offensive attitudes arise leading to disunity, which path do we choose? The Greek word translated "offense" means to trigger a trap or walk into the ". . . snare of the devil, having been taken captive by him to do his will." How many cities have seen churches split or splinter? How many splinter works were started out of division? When a church's origin is in strife, it usually reproduces strife. Once strife is resident in the DNA, only radical surgery can remove it. Usually we are in the trap because we left the place where God ordained dealing with our heart issues. Offense separates us from the very ones God ordained to help grow us up. Love covers a multitude of sin. It also can keep us in a place where our flesh gets crucified.

Are we willing to accept correction from somebody our flesh says is an adversary? Making a vessel of honor takes grace, truth and time and often considerable correction in love. How will we ever see our faults, if we do not invite our friends to speak freely to us about them? Very few Christians invite reproof. If we are serious about purifying our personal altars so there is no hindrance to covenant fulfillment when we give, we must cultivate character through reproof! **El-eng-kho** is the Greek word for correction.

Do we have any faults our closest friends can confront? **El-eng-kho** means to bring to light, to expose with correction, to admonish, call to account, reprove, rebuke, to reprehend severely, to demand an explanation. How often are we called to account? Within families, how do husbands react when wives start commenting on behavior? Sometimes its easy for wives to play the role of the Holy Spirit when no avenue of reproof is available. To be godly is to be open and approachable about one's faults. For a church to have true biblical fellowship, **el-eng-kho** must be present. How do we respond when **el-eng-kho** manifests? One enlightening exercise is to get a Greek Concordance and run the references of all the verses where **el-eng-kho** appears. (I recommend *Word Study Concordance* by Ralph Winter.) Absorbing **el-eng-kho** is a life-changing experience. Finding and reading each passage can cement this character-changing capacity in our spirit.

Proverbs 10:17 says, "He who keeps instruction is in the way of life. But he who refuses reproof goes astray." A better rendering might be "is led astray." Thank God, Jesus will leave the 99 to retrieve the one. The Hebrew word for "astray" is **taw-aw**. It means to vacillate or to be deceived. When you and I refuse reproof, we open the door for deception and captivity as the enemy springs the trap. We fall in, usually hanging in mid-air, spiritually speaking. The word picture means to be seduced. There is a very familiar passage in Isaiah 53:6 that uses this word. "All we like sheep have gone astray; . . . every one, to his own way. . . ." Dismissing a reproof or correction can cause us to move in the wrong direction. Finding fault with the reprover can signal hardness of heart. We find a fault and minimize it for the sake of peace. Peace purchased with compromise is shallow, short-lived and usually covered or coated with denial. When God sends a move of the Spirit and it is rejected because of the manifestations, we forfeit the full measure of blessing, but also open the door to deep religious deception. Religious spirits push people to kill not only the messengers but the move.

Proverbs 12:1 says, "Whoever loves instruction loves knowledge, But he who hates reproof is stupid." How is our spiritual IQ? **Bawar**, the Hebrew word translated stupid, means to be consumed by fire. It is used in Job: "The fire fell and consumed the house according to the servant. And the fire fell and consumed the sheep." Proverbs 12 indicates when we refuse reproof and correction, we open the door to fire or wither away from a lack of food. Is it possible to put ourselves in a place where God is hindered in His plans for us? Refusing correction can hinder development. What happens when we say, "I do not want to hear it"? Does God reply, "Okay, you do not have to hear it"?

Proverbs 15:10 states, "Harsh correction is for him who forsakes the way, And he who hates reproof will die." Verses 11 and 12 add, "Hell and Destruction are before the LORD; So how much more the hearts of the sons of men. A scoffer does not love one who reproves him, Nor will he go to the wise." What is the fruit of refusing reproof and correction? If not physical death, at the minimum a measure of spiritual death encroaches. We choose, often daily, how we are going to respond when reproof comes. Because God brings correction, there is nothing hidden that will not be revealed. The hidden things are usually in our hearts where attitudes hide. Circumstances and pressure come to reveal those things so we can deal with them. It is called cleansing the temple in preparation for glory. The purpose of this process is not to be miserable for another six months. The purpose is to get the temple ready for the glory of the LORD, for blessing and covenant fulfillment!

Let's look at the promises for receiving reproof. Proverbs 13:18 says, "Poverty and shame will come to him who disdains correction, But he who regards reproof will be honored." With correction comes either poverty, shame or honor, depending on our rejection or acceptance. Most of us would agree, we have had enough of poverty and shame and are ready for some honor. First Corinthians 14:23 says:

> *Therefore if the whole church comes together in one place, and all speak with tongues, and there come in those who are uninformed or unbelievers, will they not say that you are out of your mind? But if all prophesy, and an unbeliever or an uninformed person comes in, he is **el-eng-kho**/convinced by all, he is judged by all. And thus the secrets of his heart are revealed; and so, falling down on his face, he will worship God and report that God is truly among you.*

How many such manifestations have we witnessed in church? It happened in the early church; so, why not today? Perhaps God will release prophetic **el-eng-kho** through us when we demonstrate it is also welcome "to us." Why would God use us prophetically to give correction to those we do not know if we are unwilling to receive it from those we do know? On what grounds can we expect to manifest this to the world if we will not receive it from each other? When we receive, we open the door for God to pour it through us. But if we refuse to receive, we know what is going to happen if God tries to pour it through us. Pharisaism judges first, so the word comes with a cutting edge and is much harder to receive. Matthew 7 warns we cannot be used to discern and judge in someone else unless we first take the telephone pole out of our own eye. Many assume we are not to judge, but 1 Corinthians 5 rebukes believers for that misconception. To walk in authority, we have to be under authority.

Why do so many ignore this principle? Church should be a safe place to share faults and failures without fear of condemnation and criticism. There are plenty of franchise Pharisaic spiritual fast-food eateries popping up on every corner, proclaiming and presenting unsanctified prejudices. Like Paul, we must choose to know only Jesus and Him crucified. We need to wake up and realize spiritual "happy meals" digest as cheap grace. We are in a season where God wants to deal with our character. And He always starts at home, either physically or spiritually. Can we overcome offenses, humbly receive reproof and establish harmony through the love of God?

El-eng-kho appears in some very surprising places. Nearly every believer is familiar with John 3:16, "For God so loved the world that He gave His only begotten Son, that whoever believes in Him should not perish but have everlasting life." Now, what is the principle of the passage? What is the point of leaving a passage in context? Some verses are so familiar, we have lost the sense of the passage. The fruit of our religious system is taking passages we like out of context. We all know John 3:16, but what was the point of Jesus' teaching? Many think John 3:16 stands alone.

John 3:16–20 says:

> *For God so loved the world that He gave His only begotten Son, that whoever believes in Him should not perish but have everlasting life. For God did not send His Son into the world to condemn the world, but that the world through Him might be saved. He who believes in Him is not condemned; but he who does not believe is condemned already, because he has not believed in the name of the only begotten Son of God. And this is the condemnation, that the light has*

come into the world, and men loved darkness rather than light, because their deeds were evil. For everyone practicing evil hates the light and does not come to the light, **lest his deeds should be el-eng-kho**/exposed."

Coming to the light demands a willingness to be exposed. To bring to light means being exposed with conviction, to correct or call to account, to admonish, reprove, rebuke or demand an explanation. Verse 21 states, "But he who does the truth comes to the light, that his deeds may be clearly seen, that they have been done in God."

What is the point of the passage or the issue over which Jesus is dealing with those who know the covenant like Nicodemus? The point for all those who know so much is, are you willing to receive reproof and correction? If you are, you can grow in Kingdom authority in greater measure. Then Jesus lays down a principle that governs all spiritual life. Verse 20 says, ". . . Everyone practicing evil hates the light and does not come to the light, lest his deeds should be corrected." When we are not willing to deal with an attitude or a character trait, and we run from correction and reproof, this scripture describes us. Verse 21 states, "But he who does the truth comes to the light, that his deeds may be clearly seen, that they have been done in God."

What is the primary principle? What should motivate us to agree with the adversary? Spiritual prison is avoided only by those willing to run toward the light embracing exposure, correction and reproof. Are we actively cultivating this character trait? Does the church we attend pull us into the light? Or do they bless us to live in the shadows, allowing our flesh to dominate as long as we continue giving?

The Pharisees completely rejected this truth. They also paid the ultimate price. Matthew 23:25 answers: "Woe to you, scribes and Pharisees, hypocrites. For you cleanse the outside of the cup and dish, but inside they are full of extortion and self-indulgence." This describes a church experience where we are willing to attend as long as we keep God on the outside, but do not expect or demand any change on the inside. To start dealing with heart stuff, we may have to find another place to worship. ". . . You cleanse the outside of the cup and dish, but inside they are full of extortion and selfindulgence. Blind Pharisee, first cleanse the inside of the cup and dish, that the outside of them may be clean also." When we let Jesus straighten up the inside, we prepare a vessel for God's anointing, perhaps an anointing that grows out arms and legs. God is going to remove the shame of powerlessness from the church.

Verses 27–37 say:

Woe to you, scribes and Pharisees, hypocrites. For you are like whitewashed tombs which indeed appear beautiful outwardly, but inside they are full of dead men's bones and all uncleanness. Even so you also outwardly appear righteous to men, but inside you are full of hypocrisy and lawlessness. Woe to you, scribes and Pharisees, hypocrites. Because you build the tombs of the prophets and adorn the monuments of the righteous, and say, 'If we had lived in the days of our fathers, we would not have been partakers with them in the blood of the prophets.' Therefore you are witnesses against yourselves that you are sons of those who murdered the prophets. Fill up, then, the measure of your father's guilt. Serpents, brood of vipers. How can you escape the condemnation of hell? Therefore, indeed, I send you prophets, wise men, and scribes: some of them you will kill and crucify, and some of them you will scourge in your synagogues and persecute from city to city, that on you may come all the righteous blood shed on the earth, from the blood of righteous Abel to the blood of Zechariah, son of Berechiah, whom you murdered between the temple and the altar. Assuredly, I say to you, all these things will come upon this generation. O Jerusalem, Jerusalem, the one who kills the prophets and stones those who are sent to her. How often I wanted to gather your children together, as a hen gathers her chicks under her wings, but **you were not willing!** . . .

Refusing to cultivate reproof accrues a price at the altar just like attending a church built on the premise of never giving any reproof for fear of offense. Jesus could just as easily have said, "O church, church are you willing to accept reproof or correction when it uncovers a fault?" Are we willing? Willingness to accept correction is a manifestation of humility and averts judgment. Verse 38 answers, "See. Your house is left to you desolate. . . ." If spinelessness permeates pulpits, will America be left desolate? When we walk through periods of desolation, one of the best things we can do is say, "God, what do you want to deal with in my heart? I am ready to change." Verse 39 of Matthew 23 states: ". . . For I say to you, you shall see Me no more till you say, 'Blessed is He who comes in the name of the LORD!'" What did Jesus mean by that? He meant until Israel says, "Okay, Jesus, I am ready for reproof and correction." What happened in Jerusalem in A.D. 70 is a testimony to Jesus the Judge. Accepting reproof can save us and our children from untold grief. Generations who refuse the Lord may find a forfeiture of covenantal promises which transcend many generations. The history of physical Israel has not been a happy one, but the eternal promise is to make them so jealous they run to the church. A new season beckons where God has promised that the precursor of making the Jew jealous precedes grafting them back into the vine releasing a resurrection anointing. Preparation for the last great harvest is upon us. Will we utilize our time wisely and qualify for this outpouring?

Are you ready to bow
To reproof and correction?
Will you let LIGHT expose sin
With determined correction?

Will you let Jesus set straight
Any darkness inside,
So His mighty anointing
Can come and abide?

Accepting reproof
Can prevent untold grief,
A new season beckons
To REPENT brings relief.

CHAPTER 18

"JUDGMENT"

What did Jesus mean by, "Agree with your adversary . . . or you are thrown into prison. Assuredly, I say to you, you will by no means get out of there till you have paid the last penny"? Did Jesus mean what He said? Is God that fanatical about relationships? Why is He so strict about offenses? What makes God so demanding about this issue? The boundaries of the Kingdom cannot be ignored.

When leaders repent and walk according to the Word, God answers their repentance with a harvest of blessing, one of which at times is financial, unless encountering a Hebrews 10 persecution. A great end-time harvest awaits the church. Purifying the altar is a very essential part of that preparation. Year by year, the truths outlined in *Purifying the Altar* have gained acceptance. Presenting Malachi 3 without the foundation of Numbers 18:21, Matthew 5:23–24 and Matthew 23:19 is grossly unfair to any hearer and demands balancing. In Malachi 3, God challenges us to test Him by tithing while in Matthew 5, He says stop giving until we clean up our relationships, culminating in Matthew 23:19 with "purity of the altar"—then consummating the covenant and guaranteeing a blessing. This, of course, is subject to the ebb and flow of "times and seasons."

How many messages exhorting the congregation to stop giving can you remember? The main part of purifying the altar does not deal with church government. It does not deal with the proper use of tithe and offering. It deals with our relationships with each other. Which part of this equation have we emphasized? How many Malachi messages have we heard?

> *Bring all the tithes into the storehouse, and prove Me now in this' says the Lord of hosts, 'If I will not open for you the windows of heaven And pour out for you such blessing That there will not be enough room to receive it.*
>
> —Malachi 3:10

Jesus said, "**Stop**!" Do you realize what a dramatic shift of gears and change of pace that was from what we see everywhere else in the Scriptures over the issue of the covenantal promises for provision? Jesus said, "Stop this circus." No wonder the church leaders wanted to kill Him. Relationships must be important. The same God who instituted seedtime and harvest for our blessing, sustenance and provision, says if we have caused offense in the Christian family, stop the progression of giving. "If our relationships are broken, we must stop!" Why is this so important? What does it say about judgment? Luke 5:25–26 are verses explaining judgment. When Scripture talks about going into prison and not getting out until we have paid the last penny, that is a serious judgment.

And the main issue is not whether we are tithing, giving an offering, or whether we've got it distributed exactly right. The foundational issue is not whether we believe in the five-fold min-

"Judgment"

istry. The trigger for this trap can be how we get along with our mates or how we relate to our in-laws. How we get along with our kids and how we get along with the people where we work can trigger a real trap. How do we relate to our extended family and people at the church where God planted us? Are we causing waves because we disagree with leadership? God knows when we are scripturally correct there is no reason to concede. Being technically right can be financially wrong. Does evidence exist for your being financially wrong?

First Peter 4:1–2 says:

Therefore, since Christ suffered for us in the flesh, arm yourselves also with the same mind, for he who has suffered in the flesh has ceased from sin, that he no longer should live the rest of his time in the flesh for the lusts of men, but for the will of God.

Peter might have added, "I got this revelation the hard way. I want to share it with you. Here is how God delivered me from wanting to do my own thing because I had it all lined up. I knew that when Jesus defeated the Romans and became King and Lord of glory, then I would be in position to rule my own province. This whole region would be set aside for me to rule. I had it all figured out. The only problem was Jesus would not buy it. Guess how He delivered me from wanting to live for myself?" He tells us right here in context through trial, tribulation and hitting a brick wall that we are forced to change. And what is the purpose of such adversity? We must come to a place where we are willing to lower the barrier: we must say, "Alright God, here is the rest of my heart. Here is the rest of the kingdom of me, the part I have been ruling over. I am turning it over to You."

Hebrews 12:3–9 says:

For consider Him who endured such hostility from sinners against Himself, lest you become weary and discouraged in your souls. You have not yet resisted to bloodshed, striving against sin. And you have forgotten the exhortation which speaks to you as to sons; "My son, do not despise the chastening of the LORD, Nor be discouraged when you are rebuked/ **el-eng-kho** *by Him; For whom the LORD loves He chastens, And scourges every son whom He receives." If you endure chastening, God deals with you as with sons; for what son is there whom a father does not chasten? But if you are without chastening, correction, rebuke,* **el-eng-kho** *of which all have become partakers, then you are illegitimate and not sons. Furthermore, we have had human fathers who corrected us, and we paid them respect. Shall we not much more readily be in subjection to the Father of spirits and live?*

Refusing correction is an attitude of heart that forfeits the Kingdom. What must we do for God to deny us as sons and daughters? If we refuse **el-eng-kho**/correction, we are in trouble. God ordained a community, called church, probably to push every relational button that we have. Only great humility receives correction. Isn't church just wonderful? And don't we all love it? Verses 9–12 state:

Furthermore, we have had human fathers who corrected us, and we paid them respect. Shall we not much more readily be in subjection to the Father of spirits and live? For they indeed for a few days chastened us as seemed best to them but He for our profit, that we may be partakers of His holiness. Now no chastening seems to be joyful for the present, but grievous: nevertheless, afterward it yields the peaceable fruit of righteousness to those who have been trained by it. Therefore strengthen the hands which hang down, and the feeble knees, and make straight paths for your feet, so that what is lame may not be dislocated, but rather be healed."

This passage outlines the pathway to healing and deliverance. What is it called? Open your life to correction. It is God's pathway to healing and freedom. Look at verse 14, "Pursue peace. . . ." With who, we ask. Are we pursuing peace? What are we "pursuing"? Matthew 5 strongly encourages us to pursue peace.

Matthew 5:22 states:

But I say to you that whoever is angry with his brother without a cause shall be in danger of the judgment. And whoever says to his brother, "Raca!" shall be in danger of the council. But whoever says "You fool!" shall be in danger of hell fire.

God seems to send people into our lives that are like various grades of sandpaper. The more obnoxious ones are like the coarse grade designed for removing whole layers of paint and varnish along with outer layers of wood until the original core color is exposed. The issue for people in the coarse grade is not endurance but survival. If your life has decades of encounters with the coarse grade, then yield to the process so you can graduate to the medium grade sandpaper for finishing work. A medium grade of 100 grain, for those individuals who qualify, catch all the high places left by the deep gouges of the coarse. Medium sandpaper levels the road so the gouges disappear. Fine sandpaper does not remove much wood, but polishes for a very smooth feel. Do not automatically reject those who are coarse because they accomplish a purpose. Becoming like Jesus demands dealing with sandpaper people. God sends unique and unusual people to us not for our comfort but for maturity. If we can overcome the offense, then there is eternal gold to be bought in the relationship.

First John 1:5 states:

> *This is the message which we have heard from Him and declare to you that God is light and in Him is no darkness at all. If we say that we have fellowship with Him, and walk in darkness, we lie and do not practice the truth. But if we walk in the light as He is in the light, we have fellowship with one another, and the blood of Jesus Christ His Son cleanses us from all sin."*

Now why does Scripture connect "fellowship" in the church with a catalyst for cleansing from sin? Because fellowship with other believers exposes heart issues. Fellowship reveals what is really in us. We do not want it but we need it. God ordained the church as a place to grow up through multiple cleansings. God's concept of church and ours have grown apart. Church today has become a place to get a non-threatening word of encouragement in a politically correct world. Having a good time and being entertained is more important than God's Word. We dare not develop too strong a relationship with anyone or it could hinder personal freedom.

What is common in the church today could hardly compare with the book of Acts. Because of persecution, people developed relationship out of necessity—it was a life-or-death issue. What better place to do that than in a small church? Many saints hide in 500, 1,000, 5,000 or larger member churches. They never even touch the level of sandpaper relationship that cleanses. This kind of church insulates the average believer against growing in God. Verse 7 says, ". . . If we walk in the light as He is in the light, we have fellowship with one another, and the blood of Jesus Christ His Son cleanses us from all sin." This verse is a promise for the

"Judgment"

fruit of church life. It guarantees as we live with each other relationally, rub shoulders and go nose-to-nose with each other, issues are forced to the surface for cleansing. We begin to purify each other. And God says, "I planned it that way. That is the whole purpose because that is the place I have ordained for My love to flow and bring restoration and healing." God ordained relationships for cleansing, so those who grate against us the most, may be the most valuable people eternally. The coarsest sandpaper is usually found in business and family relationships. Families are populated by real characters. How did we get so blessed?

First John 2:7–10 says:

Brethren, I write no new commandment to you, but an old commandment which you have had from the beginning. The old commandment is the word which you heard from the beginning. Again, a new commandment I write to you, which thing is true in Him and in you, because the darkness is passing away, and the true light is already shining. He who says he is in the light, and fractures his relationships/ hates his brother, is in darkness until now. He who maintains his relationships/loves his brother abides in the light, and there is no cause for **skan-dal-id-zo, skan-dalon/** *offense/stumbling in him.*

We are told in Matthew, "Agree with our adversary . . ." the person we have offended. First John 2:11 counsels, "But he who destroys his relationships/hates his brother is in darkness and walks in darkness, and does not know where he is going, because the darkness has blinded his eyes." This amplifies Matthew 5 and deals with our attitude toward relationships. When God plants us in a place, whether it be a marital family or a church family or both, the purpose is to grow up. The guarantee is that someone in the mix will push every button we have causing soulish manifestations, which expose the lack of Christlikeness. The **"fight-or-flight response"** often emerges. I fight to keep my independent flesh or flee to safety in places that do not require change: divorce, work, entertainment. God often gives us relationships with family members from which there is no escape. Talk about nailing our back to the wall. In those situations, we either change or pursue a counterfeit way out ultimately producing twice the pain.

God is after Christlikeness and the path to it is not easy. Narrow is the way and few there be who find it. What is the nature of love? Most believers have heard 1 Corinthians 13 many, many times. What does it say about the love of God? Love does not fail because it does one thing. It maintains relationship. What if we have friends who are not willing to maintain relationship? We cannot force people to stay in relationship. This is true. But we can choose the path of love. Matthew 18 outlines the confrontation and restoration process where God promises covenant intervention to restore the unrepentant. Jesus the Judge knows how to intervene. As we progress toward the winding up of the age, we either prepare to represent Him or we forfeit a generational call and our children become our judges. Let the generation who authored the sexual revolution consider that.

Will we stay the course
When it doesn't feel great?
Will we deal with our "stuff"?
And set our path straight?

We need one another
To mature and to grow,
To help us with weak spots
Restoration to sow.

Maintaining connections
Will help us to bloom,
Your brother sees blind spots
For your brother make room.

CHAPTER 19

NAVIGATING A DYSFUNCTIONAL FAMILY

God ordained growth toward Christlikeness through our choices to love people in their dysfunctional state, as Jesus loved us. The personal battles are our boot camp guaranteeing growth toward maturity. The deeper we get into relationship, the more nose-to-nose encounters we face. For most of us, the greatest disagreement we face comes through those in our family.

God often draws people into marriage relationships where only breaking covenant brings relief, unless we fall on the Rock and embrace brokenness. When one of the two refuse, divorce happens. How do we bring God into the middle where He can transform us? Matthew 7 has been fractured more than once by pulling it out of context, but the passage has answers. "Judge not, that you be not judged" has to be tempered by both the context, which means do not judge as the pharisaical hypocrites, and 1

Corinthians 5 where we are rebuked for not judging. Some issues have to be discerned. God requires we take a stand based on that discernment. First Corinthians 5 deals with how we handle sin corporately. Verse 11 says:

> *But now I have written to you not to keep company with anyone named a brother, who is a fornicator, or covetous, or an idolater, or a reviler, or a drunkard, or an extortioner—not even to eat with such a person. For what have I to do with judging those also who are outside? Do you not judge those who are inside?"*

"Judge not . . ." is not a blanket application. In the early church, God dealt harshly with defiling sin. Ananias and Sapphira died suddenly. The Bible comes to us line upon line and precept upon precept. The reason we accept and implement Matthew 18 is to save people from suffering the **path** of Ananias and Sapphira. They were judged. First Corinthians 5 records a confrontation over sin that works, but today's church environment is unlikely to see it. What do we do in the meantime? Verse 11 says ". . . not even to eat with such a person."

First Corinthians 5:12–13 and 6:1–2 states:

> *For what have I to do with judging those also who are outside? Do you not judge those who are inside? But those who are outside God judges. Therefore 'put away from yourselves that wicked person/the sin.' Dare any of you, having a matter against another, go to law before the unrighteous, and not before the saints? Do you not know that the saints will judge the world? And if the world will be judged by you, are you unworthy to judge the smallest matters?*

In Matthew 7, we are rebuked for judging hypocritically, while in 1 Corinthians 5 we are rebuked for **not** judging at all. We must judge righteous judgment. Judging without following God's progression can create the wrong response. Premature judgment always creates strife. Bringing godly correction is an art to be learned. Following God's progression is the starting point. What is God's progression? There is a contextual progression clearly identified in the Sermon on the Mount demanding not only our admission but also our adherence. Matthew 6:10 starts with the issue of "giving" with a warning, "Give, but don't give like the Pharisees." Verse 5 exhorts, "Pray, but don't pray like the hypocrites." Verse 16 continues this contrast with, "Fast, but don't fast like the hypocrites." It should be understood that by the time we get to the fourth exhortation, the context is "Judge, but don't judge like the hypocrites." Jesus did not warn His hearers about not judging at all. Chapter 7, verses 2–5a says:

> *For with what judgment you judge, you will be judged; and with the same measure you use, it will be measured back to you. And why do you look at the speck in your brother's eye, but do not consider the plank in your own eye? Or how can you say to your brother, "Let me remove the speck out of your eye"; and look, a telephone pole/ plank is in your own eye? Hypocrite! . . .*

This has been taken to mean do not judge, but the remainder of Scripture on this subject demands we judge. The chief issue with judging is God does not allow hypocrisy. For example, we cannot be a plumbline to mammon if money has a hold on us. What better place for that to be resolved than family? Until mammon is under our feet, we will never qualify to execute prophetic judgment as the prophets promised. Neither will we be prepared to announce Ananias and Sapphira events if necessary. When we deal with our issues first as exhorted, "First remove the plank from your own eye, and then you will see clearly," clarity usually comes. The things which most often cloud our judgment, push our buttons or result in a nose-to-nose confrontation in the flesh, usually come from past points of pain. Confrontations in the spirit arise from transgressing boundaries of righteousness and cannot be avoided. The Ananias and Sapphira events in the future will be propelled spontaneously by the Spirit.

When we identify a wound and address the issue, clarity usually comes, freeing us to minister in the Spirit without emotional attachments. When the Lord reveals an area that contains pain from the past, we have a choice to hide or participate. God honors transparency in this process and something is birthed in our heart. It is called mercy. It is birthed because we need it, and the recognition of the need by crying out gets God's attention. And in the "crying out and receiving" of the mercy, then God does something in our hearts that enables us to "go" in a spirit of mercy. Failure to extend mercy fractures relationships. God's progression starts with us in preparation as vessels fit for the Master's use.

God is very serious about relationship, confrontation and growth through correction. Corrections are like pearls because they are spiritual doorways through which we walk if heard and accepted. Jesus proclaimed it for all to hear and see in Matthew 7:6: "Do not give what is holy to the dogs; nor cast your pearls before swine, lest they trample them under their feet, and turn and tear you in pieces." The context is correction. Godly corrections are like pearls of great value. Rather than relaying an offense to others, we should take it to the person alone. These corrections are best perfected in mother/daughter and father/son relationships. What we learn in family should be foundational for church relationships. The first discipline is in not telling others about perceived offense but going to the individual. When we choose to kill the spiritual grapevine gossip chain, real progress is being made. Using faith on our flesh to obey has great rewards. Anytime we see sin in somebody else, we should treat it as a "pearl" to be handled with care. If we do it God's way, we honor the "pearl" and it has eternal repercussions. How the receiver responds ultimately determines the outcome.

Verse 7 of Matthew 7 states: "Ask, and keep on asking and it will be given to you; seek, and keep on seeking and you will find; knock, and keep on knocking and it will be opened to you." What will be opened? Verse 8, "For everyone who asks receives. . . ." Asks for what? ". . . and he who seeks finds. . . ." Seeks what? ". . . And to him who knocks. . . ." Knocks for what? ". . . It will be opened. Or what man is there among you who, if his son asks for bread, will give him a stone? Or if he asks for a fish, will he give him a serpent?" What is the correlation? Luke 11 contains the parallel passage. The correlation is that each one of these fall into the same category.

Luke 11:11 says, "If a son asks for bread from any father among you will he give him a stone?" What is a stone? A stone is as an agent for executing judgment. Serpents were an agent of judgment for the escaping Israelites. Scorpions fell into the same category. "Or if he asks for a fish, will he give him a serpent instead of a fish? Or if he asks for an egg, will he offer him a scorpion?" What is the category of bread, fish and eggs? All three have something in common. They are all life-sustaining food. "If a son asks the father for food will the father give him judgment?" What are we talking about? What is the context of Matthew 7? The context is dealing with sin, immaturity and problems in relationships from a loving parental point of view. The bottom-line issue is, *Where are our hearts relationally when sandpaper arises?* We can either ask for food or judgment. The promise is outlined in Luke

11:13, "If you then, being evil, know how to give good gifts to your children, how much more will your heavenly Father give the Holy Spirit to those who ask Him!" The idea presented is to "ask, and keep on asking . . . seek, and keep on seeking . . . knock and keep on knocking. . . ."

How many of us after the third or fourth confrontation, give up on our children thinking they will never comprehend the change required for Christlike character. "Ask and keep on asking . . . seek, and keep on seeking . . . knock, and keep on knocking." And what is the guarantee? He will give us the measure of the Holy Spirit that is needed to bring them out of the flesh into the Spirit and into maturity. But where do we learn to be this persistent? Where do we learn to grow up in this dimension of God's heart? He ordained family which is very difficult to divorce. We can divorce mates but not brothers and sisters. God will wait years for His purposes. Does God have an answer for each of us? Yes. What is it? It is yielding the flesh to His heart and not giving up. We keep asking for the anointing of the Holy Spirit to come and break the bondage, open the eyes and enlighten the understanding. It is to plant our feet and say, "I will not quit." There is no formula that replaces following the Holy Spirit and refusing to give up. Many Christians want a far higher level of Holy Spirit anointing, but very few are willing to pay the price in patience to gain it!

In navigating family
Key moments come and go,
Corrective opportunities
To set hearts straight to grow

Will you surrender willingly
To God's "sandpaper" plan,
As Christlikeness He wants to form
In each committed man.

CHAPTER 20

THREE LEVELS OF JUDGMENTS

"Verbal Accountability"

Matthew 5:22 mentions three stages of God's accountability based on our verbal judgments. The first stage is angry words which ". . . shall be in danger of the judgment." Now the judgment that is mentioned here was the **first level** of judgment in Israel as administered by the local council in the synagogue, which in a small town had seven people in it, and they were limited in the penalty they could pass. The seven could not go as far as the seventy. There were restrictions on the seven that were not on the seventy. If we allow things to get under our skin to the point we start blasting people verbally, we are looking at level one judgment which one commentary describes as "mild strangulation." The seven could perform strangulation. That speaks to us spiritually about the flow of God which starts constricting until there is very little volume. Those wandering in a string of never-ending desert experiences could look here for a root. Repentance will eliminate this root. If the rain comes, you have found the source. If not, move to the next level.

The next level as Jesus laid it out is, "And whoever says to his brother, 'Raca!' . . ." "Raca" is a very interesting Aramaic word. It is a character judgment which contains contempt. A character judgment with contempt brings the danger of the council. The council was the Sanhedrin in Jerusalem who had the power of capital punishment/death by stoning. The **second level** is significantly more serious because the death penalty is in play. In **level three** one utters, ". . . But whoever says, 'You fool!'" The Greek word translated "fool" is **mo-ray** which comes from the word **mo-ros**. We get the word "moron" from it. It means a rebel or apostate from all good. In the third level, we condemn a person to hell. If we totally write them off when God has not written them off, then trouble ensues. We tend to do that with certain categories of people.

This level is unique because the penalty refers to the valley of Hinnom. It is the place where the wayward sacrificed their sons and daughters to Molech. It was called the valley of the living dead. It speaks of spiritual eternal loss. This understanding adds serious weight to verse 23: "Therefore if you bring your gift to the altar, and there remember that your brother has something against you. . . ." What would he have against you? He could have witnessed an outburst in one of these three areas. So if we have spoken out against somebody and they hear secondhand criticism, then we have a relational offense to address. Are we willing to take God's Word seriously? "Leave your gift there before the altar, and go your way. First be reconciled to your brother, and then come and offer your gift." Get back into the place where the covenant is operational. "Agree with your adversary quickly." Most of us believe it is better to be right. But that is not what this says. It says, "Agree with your adversary quickly, while you are on the way with him, lest the judge hand you over to the officer, and you are thrown into prison. Assuredly, I say to you, you will by no means get out of there till you have paid the last penny." Jesus initiated heavy-duty rebuke and reproof and did not spare the word with those who were destined to lead. Peter took some major confrontational hits from the Master.

James and John found Jesus to be quite blunt in His confrontation over attitudes. Jesus cares enough to confront those destined for spiritual impact. Luke 9:51–54 states:

Now it came to pass, when the time had come for Him to be received up, that He steadfastly set His face to go to Jerusalem, and sent messengers before His face. And as they went, they entered a village of the Samaritans, to prepare for Him. But they did not receive Him, because His face was set for the journey to Jerusalem. And when His disciples James and John saw this, they said, 'Lord, do You want us to command fire to come down from heaven and consume them, just as Elijah did?'

One cannot help but wonder if James and John were competing with Peter for position and power. The root of their rivalry and strife was the desire to achieve the greatest ministry. Jesus' response was verses 55–56, "But He turned and rebuked them, and said, 'You do not know what manner of spirit you are of. For the Son of Man did not come to destroy men's lives but to save them.'" God is a God of mercy, but never assume that means no judgment. It does not. Mercy for Israel demanded justice and judgment on those attempting to destroy the nation through their promotion of policies that defiled it. Those who filled the cup of iniquity were judged. As a land fills, enemies arise and are emboldened to attack. Rejecting Jesus for perversion has incurred the wrath of Islam. The covenants have not changed and therefore demand judgment. Those who oppose all war on grounds of conscience are grossly ignorant of Scripture. Treasonous retreat from fighting radical Islam only encourages the enemy. Jesus died for a victorious church who should resemble David's mighty men, instead of a band of weasels. Where are the Temple cleansers who will pay the price to transform the church?

Second Chronicles 29 describes Temple cleansing—Hebrew style. Verses 1–4 say,

> *Hezekiah became king when he was twenty-five years old, and he reigned twenty-nine years in Jerusalem. His mother's name was Abijah the daughter of Zechariah. And he did what was right in the sight of the LORD, according to all that his father David had done. In the first year of his reign, in the first month, he opened the doors of the house of the LORD and repaired them. Then he brought in the priests and the Levites, and gathered them in the East Square. . . .*

We open the door by inviting God in—some Levites choose to carry more "fullness" than others. Verses 5–7:

> *. . . And said to them: 'Hear me, Levites. Now sanctify yourselves, sanctify the house of the LORD God of your fathers, and carry out the rubbish from the holy place. For our fathers have trespassed and done evil in the eyes of the LORD our God; they have forsaken Him, have turned their faces away from the habitation of the LORD, and turned their backs on Him. They have also shut up the doors of the vestibule, put out the lamps, and have not burned incense or offered burnt offerings in the holy place of the God of Israel.'*

In other words, they closed their holy place for the dealings of God. The Senate, House and Supreme Court have done exactly that to the nation. They have locked God out. They have banned Him from schools and public meetings. Will God anoint priests for judgment to carry out the real garbage, which is every leader hostile to God? Let the anointing to remove national garbage arise. From nation to nation, political leaders are being forced to choose to accept or reject God's Word. By statutorily protecting homosexuality, these leaders openly reject God's standard and guarantee judgment on the nation. When the New Testament church prayed, as spiritual kings—angels were sent with the answer and corrupt king Herod was eaten alive. Jesus is the same yesterday, today and forever. It is time to pray as kings and let the angels visit the enemies. (For explicit prayers see *The Sure Mercies of David*.)

A clash of governments exist where political position promotes a perverse agenda demanding God's people bow to it. A parallel confrontation occurred during the ministry of Elijah recorded in 2 Kings 1:9–11:

> *Then the king sent to him a captain of fifty with his fifty men. So he went up to him; and there he was, sitting on the top of a hill. And he spoke to him; 'Man of God, the king has said, "Come down!"' So Elijah answered and said to the captain of fifty, 'If I am a man of God, then let fire come down from heaven and consume you and your fifty men.' And fire came down from heaven and consumed him and his fifty. Then he sent to him another captain of fifty with his fifty men. And he answered and said to him: "Man of God, thus has the king said, 'Come down quickly!'"*

The Lord took me to this passage and retranslated it comparing what the church now faces to what Elijah faced. The key is the king's command: "Man of God come down." The Hebrew word **yah-rad** demands subservience, but God rarely allows His people to submit to demons—the biblical response is to cast them out or at least confront them. Elijah's response says, "If I represent the government of God, let fire '**yah-rad**'." Each time the king demanded the spokesman for God's government **yah-rad** or bow in worship, God turned the king's command into judgment on his own emissaries. Each time the king issued a **yah-rad**, God brought that **yah-rad** back on the king. When governments (local, state or national) pass laws protecting abortion or criminalizing as hate speech what the Bible says about homosexuality, then they in effect issue a **yah-rad** to God's representatives. Like Elijah, we must demand Divine intervention. We do that with the king's anointing through prayer. Acts 5:17–20 records God's heart on the issue of silencing the church:

> *Then the high priest rose up, and all those who were with him (which is the sect of the Sadducees), and they were filled with indignation, and laid their hands on the apostles and put them in the common prison. But at night an angel of the Lord opened the prison doors and brought them out, and said, 'Go, stand in the temple and speak to the people all the words of this life.'*

God demands we speak His words in the face of all threats therefore we must prepare the church to covenantally demand the justice of God on those issuing governmental **yah-rads**. The early church prayed and Herod was removed (see *The Sure Mercies of David*—Part II). We are not calling fire down on leaders but we, like Elijah, have the responsibility of warning them that what they propose against God's revealed will, like homosexuality and abortion, will come upon them until their seed (sons and daughters) are removed from the earth. Every leader who champions homosexuality risks seeing that perversion fall upon their own children. The same principle now applies to abortion. As we plead with leaders not to champion what destroys a nation, we must warn them of God's willingness to abort their desires. God's government is available to the church. If we will proclaim it, God will back it up. Why should the wrath of God fall on the nation bringing everincreasing calamity? Why should the history of Israel repeat itself?

Second Chronicles 29:8–11 states:

Therefore the wrath of the LORD fell upon Judah and Jerusalem, and He has given them up to trouble, to astonishment, and to jeering, as you see with your eyes. For indeed, because of this our fathers have fallen by the sword; and our sons, our daughters, and our wives are in captivity. Now it is in my heart to make a covenant with the LORD God of Israel, that His fierce wrath may turn away from us. My sons, do not be negligent now, for the LORD has chosen you to stand before Him, to serve Him, and that you should minister to Him and burn incense (to walk with Him in this season).

Qualifying to Execute Covenant Justice

We cannot impact political leadership until we clean up the church.

They got up and began to move with God. Second Chronicles 29:15–16 state:

And they gathered their brethren, sanctified themselves, and went according to the commandment of the king, at the words of the LORD, to cleanse the house of the LORD. Then the priests went into the inner part of the house of the LORD to cleanse it, and brought out all the debris that they found in the temple of the LORD to the court of the house of the LORD. And the Levites took it out and carried it to the Brook Kidron.

The fire was there along with the sacrificial stone which sits in the Dome of the Rock. It is right there on the temple ground. The blood of the sacrifice drained out into the valley of Hinnom. This is a picture of how they took each other's shame to the fire for cleansing. They carried each other's sin. They took all the debris they found in the Holy of Holies and in the Holy Place and they took it out and put it under the blood. They did not criticize each other with it. They did not scar each other with it. They did not cut each other with it. They took it out and covered it in blood and applied mercy. Guess what happened in Israel? The next five chapters declare unparalleled blessing that resulted from their actions!

Second Chronicles 30:27 states: "Then the priests, the Levites, arose and blessed the people, and their voice was heard; and their prayer came up to His holy dwelling place, to heaven."

Chapter 31, verses 9–10 say:

Then Hezekiah questioned the priests and the Levites concerning the heaps. And Azariah the chief priest, from the house of Zadok, answered him and said, "Since the people began to bring the offerings into the house of the LORD, we have had enough to eat and have plenty left, for the LORD has blessed His people; and what is left is this great abundance."

God brought great prosperity. Sennacherib, king of Assyria, came to steal it. Hezekiah prayed an imprecatory Davidic prayer.

God put a hook in Sennacherib's jaw and took him away. One hundred eighty-five thousand enemy soldiers died in one night because the king prayed "against" the enemy. Have we prayed against those defiling our nation? You could not be an enemy of covenant Israel and live. We serve the same God. He is the same yesterday, today and forever. Let the same angel execute the same judgment. Cleansing the Temple moves God's hand personally, locally and nationally. A failure to pray is a failure to move God's hand and is a failure to save the nation!

Chapter 32, verses 27–30 records:

Hezekiah had very great riches and honor. And he made himself treasuries for silver, for gold, for precious stones, for spices, for shields, and for all kinds of desirable items; storehouses for the harvest of grain, wine, and oil; and stalls for all kinds of livestock, and folds for flocks. Moreover he provided cities for himself, and possessions of flocks and herds in abundance; for God had given him very much property. This same Hezekiah also stopped the water outlet of Upper Gihon, and brought the water by tunnel to the west side of the City of David. Hezekiah prospered in all his works.

What can we say about what God did for Israel, once they cleansed the house of the LORD? We have chapter upon chapter upon chapter of blessing, blessing, blessing, blessing, blessing. Why? Because they were willing to carry each other's shame, debris, sin, garbage to the brook Kidron and cover it with the blood. Will the church grow up and rise to the occasion in dealing with internal faults and failures so we can confront the enemy?

Temple Cleansing Exposure

Matthew 27 describes a chain of events which depict a progression which parallels what is currently unfolding in the church world. Matthew 27:50 says, "Jesus, when He had cried out again with a loud voice, yielded up His spirit. And behold, the veil of the temple was torn in two from top to bottom; and the earth quaked, and the rocks were split. . . ." The thick curtain guarding the Holy of Holies was now wide open. I believe we are entering a season of great grace where the barrier is being opened for judicial access. Where was that curtain physically located? Between the Holy Place and the Holy of Holies. Why did God tear that curtain in two? It signified removal of impediment. There was another issue. When that curtain was torn in two, everyone could see the total absence of an ark. Herod's temple was arkless. The curtain was there to separate people from the glory of God and the presence of God because it would consume them if they were not properly prepared.

Historians think Jeremiah hid the ark just before 587 B.C. when Jerusalem was destroyed by Nebuchadnezzar. When Jesus died, God tore the curtain in two so He could show everyone a religious system without any content. There was no ark behind the curtain. The holiest of all was empty. The ark came into Jerusalem riding on two donkeys and they rejected the ark of God. And when they rejected the ark of God and crucified Him, God said, "Alright, I am going to show you what is really in your religious system—rip—behold an empty room!" There was nothing present in the old form. Everything had been invested in a Person Who demanded relationship. God had become flesh, forever changing worship. God demanded relationship!

God plants us in places where people push our buttons to see who occupies our personal Holy of Holies. Our curtains are being torn in two. And we are finding out how much of God we have in the Holy of Holies. We are His temple, but how much of us is there locking Him out? God gets locked out through fear, pain, shame and devastation. When God rips a curtain, there is no possible repair. How much of God is in our Holy of Holies? Ephesians 4:13 makes five-fold ministry responsible for growing the church to the "fullness of Christ." Colossians 2:9–10 says, "For in Him dwells all the fullness of the Godhead bodily; and you are complete in Him, who is the head of all principality and power." The Greek word translated "complete" is the action form of the same word translated "fullness." Jesus is our resident Ark. Purifying the altar starts at home. How much of God is in our Holy of Holies? Only a ripped curtain or crucified life reveals the answer. ". . . Arise . . . to Your resting place, You and the ark of Your strength!" (2 Chronicles 6:41). This is the prayer of the broken, humble and obedient that God answers through mercy. Make it your prayer!

We are God's own temples
Have we welcomed Him in?
Toward His workings and dealings
Let the cleansing begin.

May we humbly offer
All the junk and debris
To be dealt with and mended
Doing so willingly.

*A season of **great grace***
It is here at the door,
*Let us **purify altars***
For what is in store.

CHAPTER 21

THE POWER OF THE PURIFIED ALTAR

Genesis 35:1–5 spells out the preparational path and ultimate power available from doing business with God at a purified altar:

> *Then God said to Jacob, 'Arise, go up to Bethel and dwell there; and make an altar there to God, who appeared to you when you fled from the face of Esau your brother.' And Jacob said to his household and to all who were with him, 'Put away the foreign gods that are among you, purify yourselves, and change your garments. Then let us arise and go up to Bethel; and I will make an altar there to God, who answered me in the day of my distress and has been with me in the way which I have gone.' So they gave Jacob all the foreign gods which were in their hands, and all their earrings which were in their ears; and Jacob hid them under the terebinth tree*

which was by Shechem. And they journeyed, **and the terror of God** *was upon the cities that were all around them, and they did not pursue the sons of Jacob.*

Jacob was called to return to the place of his original vow where tithing was established and renew the covenant by building an altar.

The church has been walking for a long time without the terror of the Lord in manifestation. When the church refuses to pay the price for the terror of the Lord, we open the door for demons to terrorize us from a counterfeit religion. Jacob understood God's requirements: 1) Put away foreign gods dealt with idolatry. 2) Purify yourselves was satisfied by removing gold ornaments which speaks of separating from the spirit of mammon. 3) The change of garments signified denying the dictates of the flesh.

The foundation of the altar had to be laid with pure hands. The willingness to yield to God's requirements brought a heavenly response which should be available today. God's response brought the terror of the Lord upon all their enemies. Shall we not expect the same thing as we begin to purify again the altars of God? To see the power and promises expected from a purified altar, we return to Genesis 28 and Jacob's very first encounter where God initiated the entire process. Genesis 28:11 says:

> *So he came to a certain place and stayed there all night, because the sun had set. And he took one of the stones of that place and put it at his head, and he lay down in that place to sleep.*

The Hebrew word translated in verse 11 "came to a certain place" is the Hebrew word **paw-gah**. It has two basic meanings which are 1) "to intercede" and 2) "to lay, burdened." It specifically speaks to the intersection of man's physical path with divine purpose. **Paw-gah** describes the place where, often through no specific intent of our own, we run headfirst into the brick wall of God's eternal purpose. Regardless of the circumstances of our birth or condition of our life, an omniscient God knew us in the womb and has an eternal purpose contributing to His plan. Do we know that purpose? How do we find it? Giving into a pure altar promises a path revealing God's "before the foundation of the earth" purpose. Every individual has a right to know God's eternal purpose for which they will give an account at the White Throne of Judgment. Pure altars release eternal purpose. If you do not know, change the place you sow!

Many Christian leaders develop their faith to gain what they want. When giving at their altars, the flesh is strengthened to pursue personal gratification at the expense of "eternal purpose." When giving at a pure altar, our spirits are strengthened to use our faith on our flesh to obey God by denying self in pursuit of heaven's ultimate goal. Ministers will be held accountable for establishing an altar where it is man's desires instead of God's that are strengthened. Without the three steps of Genesis 35, Jacob would have built impurity into the altar strengthening the flesh in all who worshipped there. May God save us from participating in that which perverts and hinders Holy Spirit pursuits!

The origin of an altar is critical in establishing the full measure of promises that follow Jacob's encounter. If the origin of an altar is in strife, division or separation such as a church split, then strife, division and separation are strengthened in all who give there. If those issues are not addressed and healed, then those who sow into that altar open their lives to the same strife, division and separation that founded the altar. If the origin of an altar is in God's purity, it guarantees reproduction of God's heart and character in those who give. If our heavenly relational interaction is hindered, one place to quickly check is the origin of the altar to which we consistently sow. A purified altar guarantees relational interaction with God. God talks and He directs. Do not forfeit it!

Genesis 28:13 indicates covenant promises are generationally reactivated at purified altars. God had already covenantally promised the land to Abraham and his descendents. Our Bible is full of covenantal promises for fulfilling eternal purpose. A purified altar guarantees access to those covenant promises. Will we gravitate toward the promises of personal blessing or will we pursue the promises of Christlike character (as portrayed in both the Gospels and Revelation)? Sowing into a pure altar should expedite 2 Peter 1:2–4 in our lives:

> *Grace and peace be multiplied to you in the knowledge of God and of Jesus our Lord, as His divine power has given to us all things that pertain to life and godliness, through the knowledge of him who called us by glory and virtue, by which have been given to us exceedingly great and precious promises, that through these you may be partakers of the divine nature, having escaped the corruption that is in the world through lust.*

The promises of provision are temporary but developing character is eternal.

Verse 15 opens the gate to a third promise of God's keeping presence regardless of the level of adversity that might be encountered. Jacob encountered significant adversity. His father-inlaw wanted to steal everything he gained. He faced adversity in the magnitude of encountering people who were determined to kill him. When purification is present, the terror of God falls upon demonized people and they are rendered powerless. It is absolutely essential that the church open this gate for every believer who walks in the last days. Where we sow determines the flow!

The fourth promise of a purified altar in verse 15 of Genesis 28 is, ". . . I will keep you . . ." or give you access to a portal of provision. Failure to open the windows of heaven is the rampant fruit of impure altars. God's covenant of provision is as good as His covenant of salvation. Access to them of any magnitude can generate tremendous resistance. Abraham saw great warfare but God redeemed even his mistakes and blessed him in the process. God demonstrated His power of provision through Abraham.

Finally, in verse 17 a pure altar opens a path for receiving God's guidance. It is one thing to have a promise. It is quite another thing to activate it, believe for it and call it into existence. It is certainly incumbent upon us to inquire of the Lord and make sure that what we are giving gains us access to the full measure of covenant that is promised. Pure altars sanctify what is given, consummate the covenant and ignite the promise. One way to save ourselves from impure altars is to stop giving by ***apparent*** need where manipulation is rampant. Give only by ***revealed*** need as the Holy Spirit directs. [The apostles advised in the Didache, "Let thine alms sweat into thine hands, until thou shalt have learnt to whom to give." [15] When God moves us to give, we know it is right and He is responsible for the condition of the altar.

Those who have the responsibility of managing a corporate charitable trust or directing institutional giving owe it to God to do their due diligence on the places where they give. Giving large gifts to many of our universities and colleges today does nothing more than fuel the destruction of a generation by empowering the "progressives" to edit out our Christian history and advance their Anti-Christ agenda! Sowing into generational treason deserves an

---

15. *The Apostolic Fathers* by J. B. Lightfoot, edited and completed by J. R. Harmer. Baker Book House, Grand Rapids, MI, copyright July 1956. Reprinted from the "Apostolic Fathers" 1871 by MacMillan & Company, London.

eternal grave. Just throwing money at a problem does not cure it. Handling money demands wisdom—the kind that should flow from a pure altar!

Jacob's response to what God promised was to give a tenth to Him. Jacob vowed to give a tithe if God would meet five basic needs: 1) ". . . be with me . . ."; 2) ". . . keep me . . ." or cut off my enemies; 3) ". . . give me bread . . ."; 4) ". . . clothing . . ." or shelter; and 5) "come back . . . in peace . . ." or fulfill my calling. In 2 Samuel 7:9 where God meets David to offer a covenant of "Sure Mercy," He reminds David of the tithing provisions already fulfilled, "And I have been **with you** wherever you have gone, and have **cut off** all your enemies from before you. . . ." In Genesis 35, God demanded Jacob purify himself and build an altar. The fruit of purification follows. If the church will rise up and purify our altars, then once again we will see the fullness of God's covenant and His judicial terror on the enemies in the land. The choice is up to us. If we are not getting access to the promises, we must ask the Lord to lead us to an altar that will grant them. Representing a covenant-keeping God demands we first keep covenant. May the **"terror of the Lord"** be restored to the church! and to every tither!

Let us pursue what God pursues
With hearts and altars rendered pure,
With eyes wide open unto Truth,
And ears that fully, deeply hear.

God's promises come forth fulfilled
Eternal purpose is released,
And holy throne-room strategies
Then come to pass with fruit increased.

CHAPTER 22

HOW STRONG CHRISTIANS GROW WEAK

In Matthew 24, when the disciples asked Jesus what it would be like at the end of the age, the first thing He offered was a colossal warning, "Take heed that no one deceives you." According to Jesus, the greatest war we will fight in the end-times is between discernment and deception. Discerning right from wrong is a function of knowing God's Word and walking in the Spirit. Hebrews 4:12 says, "The 'word of God is . . . a discerner of the thoughts and intents of the heart." Hebrews 5:14 adds, "But solid food belongs to those who are of full age, that is, those who by reason of use have their senses exercised [trained] to discern both good and evil." When a car engine runs out of oil, it seizes. When a Christian's Word level is three quarts low, their discernment seizes. We should all be checking our spiritual dipsticks. The failure to apply diligence in allocating time to refuel our engine with

God's Word leads to weakness. Prioritizing our time to honor the Word guarantees growth and maintains strength. Allowing our time in the Word to slip is like depriving our car engine of oil and it marks a deterioration in the output of spiritual horsepower. It is often the first way we begin losing strength.

A second way strong Christians grow weak is that they, like Thyatira, begin to grow tolerant of what God abhors! Tolerating evil carries a very heavy penalty in the last days! The demonic doctrine of tolerance has gained a great foothold in the church. When evil reaches epidemic proportions, God historically judges it and the nations embracing it cease to exist. Judicial decisions that promote evil by legislating it from the bench are very troubling for this reason. Judicial activism has dismantled legal barriers which protected the nation against divine judgment. God does not tolerate evil indefinitely—He judges it!

The fear of judging has neutered the church and is another misapplication of God's Word. First Corinthians 12:31 commands us, "But earnestly desire the best [greater] gifts." While working of miracles and gifts of healings are the most sought after to ease pain, the best gift is the one we need the most. Discerning of spirits may well grow into that place for the end-time church. When deception grows to its current level, discerning is God's antidote. Deception is eating up the church at a rate that is astounding to many of us who grew up in a generation where we chose to accept biblical prohibitions. When my generation started its Christian experience, none of us ever dreamed that we would see a day when denominational churches would ordain homosexual priests or bless same-sex unions. The Bible was given enough reverence that we believed what scripture said. That may be the only sense that our generation was not that different from the one that founded the nation.

Many nations have a Godly heritage from forefathers who

believed what the Bible said and acted on it! They cried out to the God of Abraham, Isaac and Jacob and He answered them. America is one of many nations that exist because Jesus Christ is the only way to God and prayer works. We find ourselves rapidly losing a nation but that is only possible if God first loses the church in that nation.

The LORD encouraged me one day by saying, "If I answered the prayers of the founding generation to birth this nation, do you not think I will answer your generation's prayers to save it?" Their prayers were against the greatest military power of the then known world and God answered! Our prayers must arise against the greatest advance of evil since Sodom and Gomorrah. Because the church only knows layer one of God's love, our prayers often enable the enemy instead of bringing the full weight of God's judicial Throne upon them. Judicial prayers are offered for repentance and salvation. Every true Christian loves each person caught in the deception that they were born perverse. Sin is a choice that every person makes and through Christ, we offer grace to every individual. Leviticus 20 identifies the statutorial protection of abortion, new age, drugs and homosexuality as culprits that deprive a nation of the ability to defend itself. Homosexual marriage is not about civil rights. It is about closing churches and silencing opposing voices. Only radical homosexuals have targeted the destruction of churches through a strategy of legalizing homosexual marriage and then penalizing churches with discrimination lawsuits for refusing to marry them. Covenant mercy to the righteous means death and destruction to the enemy. David understood that and prayed accordingly. The Jesus of Revelation has no problem executing Justice. Jesus loves mankind enough to judge the evil among us! God's love kills when necessary to save. God told Pharoah, ". . . let my son go that he may serve me. But if you refuse to let him go, I will kill your son, your firstborn." The Jesus of Revelation judges evildoers who refuse to repent!

When Jesus said, "Take heed that no one deceives you," He was prophesying what the main battle would be in the last days. Any time we depart from Scripture, we open the door to deception. Deuteronomy 4:1–3 outlines the principle, often violated today, that leads many to lose discernment.

> *Hear now O Israel, the decrees and laws I am about to teach you. Follow them so that you may live and may go in and take possession of the land that the Lord the God of your fathers, is giving you. Do not add to what I command you and do not subtract from it, but keep the commands of the Lord your God that I give you. You saw with your own eyes what the LORD did at Baal Peor. The LORD your God destroyed from among you everyone who followed the Baal of Peor. . . .*

This reference is to sexual sin where everyone who participated was killed that day. God can be pushed into a position of zero tolerance. When that moment arrives, whole cities will probably be destroyed. By promoting homosexuality in the classroom from kindergarten to college and in the military, America's leaders are pushing God into a zero tolerance corner and the fruit will be devastating. Moses warned Israel that they were not to **add** to nor **take away** from Scripture. Emphasizing Jesus the Savior while neglecting Jesus the Judge comes dangerously close. Statutorily protecting homosexuality by judicial fiat should have the Church demanding covenant intervention. The Jesus of Revelation loves His creation enough to destroy those defiling it. Revelation reveals a Jesus who kills more than He saves at the end of the age. Sin can quickly cause a people to depart from the standard that God gave. Since Jesus Christ is the same yesterday, today and forever, He does not change. There is not a shadow of turning in

Him. He judges today by the same standard—which is His Word! When the culture begins to resemble Sodom and Gomorrah, we can expect parallel devastation!

How can the church turn so quickly from the Commandments given and embrace perversion? The answer is in this early warning that Moses gave. Do not add to Scripture and do not take away. We are watching the fruit of both adding/overemphasizing one truth—the first layer of God's love—while refusing to teach the last layer of love where He judges.

It seems the answer then should be obvious: reclaiming Jesus the Judge is the only way to both restore the Church and the nation. The same God who destroyed those at Baal Peor, who fell for Baalam's temptation, has not changed. If the same Jesus who visited Ananias and Sapphira started visiting churches today, who would be carried out and who would be saved? Acts 5 records a resurrected, Holy Christ judging sin in the camp as He came to church. Mercy to a nation means the destruction of those defiling it, especially arrogant judges who think they can impose their will on people! When the Jesus of Revelation visits judges, even their memory will perish—come quickly Lord Jesus! Psalm 2:10–12 speaks directly to judges when it says,

> *. . . Be instructed you judges of the earth. Serve the Lord with fear, and rejoice with trembling. Kiss the Son, lest He be angry, And you perish in the way, when His wrath is kindled but a little.*

Current judicial decisions are kindling quite a biblical bonfire! Deuteronomy 12:29–32 brings another warning when it says,

> *When the Lord your God cuts off from before you the nations which you go to dispossess, and you displace them and dwell*

> *in their land, take heed to yourself that you are not ensnared to follow them, after they are destroyed from before you, and that you do not inquire after their gods, saying, "How did these nations serve their gods? I also will do likewise." You shall not worship the LORD your God in that way; for every abomination to the LORD which He hates they have done to their gods; for they burn even their sons and daughters in the fire to their gods [abortion]. "Whatever I command you, be careful to observe it; you shall not add to it nor take away from it."*

We have the fruit of violating this scripture. Deceived denominations broadcast their apostasy by their actions in ordaining homosexual priests. Will God judge these deviant priests? How can the believing church respond to this overwhelming onslaught of evil? Asking Jesus to visit seems to be the only answer! Come Lord Jesus!

A third way strong Christians grow weak is choosing to attend churches that minimize the Word. In Jeremiah 26:1–3 we have God outlining for Jeremiah the reason that he must speak every word that God gives him, and the consequences of what will happen if he does not. It says,

> *In the beginning of the reign of Jehoiakim the son of Josiah, king of Judah, this word came from the LORD, saying, "Thus says the LORD: 'Stand in the court of the LORD's house, and speak to all the cities of Judah, which come to worship In the LORD's house, all the words that I command you to speak to them. Do not diminish a word. Perhaps everyone will listen and turn from his evil way that I may relent concerning the calamity which I purpose to bring on them because of the evil of their doings.'"*

There is a ministry model today prevailing in many nations called "Seeker-sensitive Christianity," where a choice is made not to address controversial issues like abortion, homosexuality or do anything to offend people we want to eventually win. The real question is, when we win them, what have we won? We certainly have not won a disciple. We may not even have a convert. Jesus made it clear to the early disciples that if they were not willing to die for Him, they were not His disciples at all. A watered-down Gospel produces half-hearted converts and weasel Christianity results.

Many churches seem to be offering a very cheap salvation because it requires nothing of its hearers; consequently, we have a watered-down wimpy Christianity that doesn't stand for anything because it doesn't know anything. When a person sits continually in a seeker-sensitive church, the meal they get is less than baby food. In the natural, no infant could ever grow up and develop physically while being continually malnourished. Some of the worst pictures of starvation in third-world countries are actually quite defining of well-fed believers in the natural who plop themselves down and get a thimble of nice, sweet Jesus every Sunday and never grow up in their spirit. Their spirit-man looks like the malnourished pictures we see out of third-world countries where people are starving. There is no spiritual strength, very little integrity because the Word "diet" has been diminished, diminished, **diminished**.

Moses warned twice, "Do not diminish the Word." Jeremiah was warned twice by God: "Do not diminish the Word." And yet today, our largest churches operate on the principle of diminishing the Word. Even if you are a strong Christian and consistently sit under that, you will grow weak. It is inevitable and you cannot escape it. You can be proud of your 50,000, 20,000, or 10,000 person-church, but when your diet is diminished, you are growing weak in your ability to represent Jesus. Representing Jesus as the Judge of all the earth is the only way we can save nations. The more a Christian participates in a compromised altar, the weaker he becomes!

Without faith it is impossible to please God. Hebrews 11 says, "By faith Abraham . . . by faith Enoch . . . By faith Noah . . . By faith Isaac . . . By faith Jacob . . . By faith . . . Joseph . . . By faith Moses . . . By faith the walls of Jericho. . . ." Faith always leaves what is safe and walks in risk! Faith embraces the Kingly Christ who judges and makes war. Hebrews 11:33–34 says of the prophets,

> *Who through faith subdued kingdoms, worked righteousness, obtained promises, stopped the mouths of lions, quenched the violence of fire, escaped the edge of the sword, out of weakness were made strong, became valiant in battle, turned to flight the armies of the aliens.*

It is impossible for faith to retreat to safety when a battle for the land looms.

The fourth way that strong Christians grow weak is that they choose safety over risk. Many in the church today find themselves willfully ignorant and unprepared for what is unfolding in the land. It takes a certain level of dysfunction to continually choose a spiritual restaurant that only serves salad. When a Christian chooses safety and convenience, compromise usually follows. At this point, we are trapped and disconnected from the power supply. Faith always follows God even when it takes us out of our comfort zone!

A fifth level of weakness develops when we continually sow into a compromised altar. In Matthew 23:19 Jesus said, "Fools and blind! For which is greater, the gift or the altar that sanctifies the gift?" In God's economy, we become one with the altar to which we sow. If there is compromise or diminishing of the Word in the altar to which we sow, then there is a spirit of compromise and diminishing of the Word that slowly begins to grow in our life until we find ourselves in the place that other things overtake our time in Scripture. We just lose our motivation to feed ourselves because we go for a pleasant environment with a comfortable atmosphere. After all, we don't want to offend anybody. The demonic doctrine of tolerance takes hold until we are denying Jesus and apostate by approving what He abhors! What was unthinkable growing up in the Methodist, Episcopalian, Lutheran and Presbyterian churches is now an apostate reality. How could this happen to once honorable witnesses for Jesus?

Jesus said, "Woe to you when all men speak good of you." The most famous quote in Scripture that shows us what happens when we sow into impurity is in 1 Kings 12, where Jeroboam devised construction of an altar without God's direction and was quickly confronted by the Lord with dramatic judgment. The most interesting part of the story is the condition of the old prophet who chases the young prophet after he delivers a judicial Word declaring destruction on the altar. The old prophet lies to the young man and tells him that an angel has spoken to him and he is supposed to come back to the old prophet's house and eat bread and drink water. The original assignment was to deliver the Word, and whatever you do, do not eat bread or drink water in the place of impurity around the defiled altar. Because when you do, what is in the altar gets in you. That was how God instructed the young prophet. But the young prophet erred in listening to the old prophet. He turned around, came back and ate. The old prophet got a Word from the Lord and confronted the young prophet. He told him that because he disobeyed the Word of the Lord, he would die.

Most believers who read this passage have the same reaction:

"God, this is totally unfair to the young prophet." But the young prophet is in disobedience. The young prophet is eating bread and drinking water in a defiled place. Now the interesting thing to ask is, how can the old prophet give a good word of the Lord out of one side of his mouth, and out of the other, lie without seemingly any conscience? The old prophet now has become exactly like the altar where he fellowships. The spirit of the man who built the altar has been reproduced in the old prophet. The rebellion that was in the man who built the altar is now fully operational in the old prophet and it causes the death of the young prophet. What we sow into is what we become. Every time we put an offering or a tithe on an altar, then what God put in that altar is supposed to grow and develop in us. God ordained that principle for our blessing, growth and development. It is absolutely essential that those in charge of the altar do not diminish the Word. If they choose to diminish the Word then their compromise begins to reproduce in every individual who supports or sows into that altar. Sowing into a denominational congregation that is supporting the ordaining of homosexual bishops opens up your life to perversion and every member of your family living under your roof. How deceived are we not to see that? And yet it happens every single day. Strong Christians grow weak when they sow into impurity and impurity begins to grow and transform them separating them from their source of power and authority! Some Christians sow into their own destruction! Do not be one of them!

The sixth way Christians grow weak is they participate in bloodguiltiness. Perhaps there is no greater issue in Scripture than the shedding of innocent blood. It is a divider in both the Old and New Testaments. In Genesis 4:10 God said to Cain, "The voice of your brother's blood cries out to Me from the ground." In Deuteronomy 19:10, it says, "lest innocent blood be shed in the midst of your land which the LORD your God is giving you as an inheritance, and thus guilt of bloodshed [bloodguiltiness] be upon you." Verse 13 says of the one who sheds innocent blood, "Your eye shall not pity him, but shall put away the guilt of innocent blood from Israel, that it may go well with you."

Revelation 16:6 proves the New Testament treats the shedding of innocent blood the same way, indicating that nothing has changed in God's judgment on this issue from the Old to the New covenants. "For they have shed the blood of saints and prophets, And You have given them blood to drink. For it is their just due." Strong Christians grow weak when they covenant with those who further the shedding of innocent blood in the land. The first way that usually happens to believers is when they vote. Every single Christian who voted for a Democrat or Republican who supports abortion stands under the curse of bloodguiltiness, and either repents for their vote or will consistently grow weak. God appointed individuals who were designated as "blood avengers" in the Old Covenant. They roamed the land looking for those who shed innocent blood in order to kill them. The shedding of innocent blood brought a curse on the guilty party and on the land where the event occurred. There was a specific prescription for cleansing the land. Cities of Refuge were created for perpetrators who accidently shed innocent blood. If we support those who willfully shed innocent blood we share in their punishment. The issue is: are we in any way joining ourselves to the shedding of innocent blood? Are we deceived because the Word has been diminished in our lives? Do we believe a Christian must be tolerant? Do we believe Christ belongs in the church but not in the state? Have we bought these deceptions? To vote for a politician who supports abortion is to accrue innocent blood to our hands and to think that we can grow strong in the Lord and represent Him while blood is on our hands is the epitome of deception. Christians who vote for those who support abortion sow into their own spiritual destruction! There has been an erosion in the pattern of sound doctrine necessary to keep us Christ-centered. Preaching only the Savior while neglecting Jesus the Judge is Christ-corrupting. Bloodguiltiness is real. It is every bit as real in the New Testament as it was in the Old. It is defiling, it is destroying and no one who names himself a believer can afford it.

One of the best friends that I had in the ministry, Don Weber, is now in heaven. Just before this last presidential election, he got a word from the Lord that shows us God's perspective of what happens when we vote. This is what he said,

> The vote you cast is not just a vote, it is seed. It will lead to a harvest. Many have said I will judge the land and many words will be released. I am not judging the land, **I am going to judge the votes. Votes are seed. Be not deceived, God is not mocked. As a man sows so shall he reap (Galatians 6:7).**
>
> If My people voted for economic reasons, they sowed into mammon and will harvest the unrighteous impact of mammon on their lives and financial picture.
>
> If My people voted for peace issues they have put their faith in strength of man and not the power of My word.
>
> If My people voted for unrighteous laws (abortion, murder called suicide, gay rights) contrary to My Word they have sown in unrighteousness. People who voted for assisted suicide have released a spirit of murder suicide against their land, their families. People who voted against My Word on marriage have sown into the destruction of their own families.
>
> If My people voted for racial reasons on either side they have opened the doors to be judged the same way.
>
> If My People voted in righteousness they have sown

into righteousness and will harvest it as well. Isaiah 32:17 says, ". . . The work of righteousness shall be peace and the harvest of righteousness quietness and assurance forever."

My kingdom is not a place of voting, it is a place My Word and spiritual authority rule. I formed nations where people can vote so they can make and sow a seed, a vote of righteousness of My Word.

There is a seventh way strong Christians can grow weak. Bloodguiltiness can accrue to us by going to Church. Ezekiel 3:18 forms the foundation for an insidious deception in today's church, robbing many Christians of their covenantal foundation before the Throne and slowly rendering strength into weakness. Verse 18 defines the law of the watchman,

> *When I say to the wicked, 'You shall surely die,' and you give him no warning, nor speak to warn the wicked from his wicked ways, to save his life, that same wicked man shall die in his iniquity; but his blood I will require at your hand.*

When ministers adopt a ministry model of seeker-sensitivity, where they refuse to confront sin for fear of offending, they accrue bloodguiltiness rapidly. Everyone who sows into the altar partakes of that sin of compromise and participates in the bloodguiltiness of those choices, slowly taking them from strength to weakness, biblical discernment disappears until they judge good as evil and evil as good. For all those who say that this does not apply in the New Testament, they must explain away Paul's word in Acts 20:26–27, "Therefore I testify to you this day that I am innocent of the blood of all men, For I have not shunned to declare to you the whole counsel of God."

Paul believed the law of the watchman was still operational in the New Testament. Every dollar sown into the average seeker-sensitive altar produces a harvest of compromise in the sower until their discernment is gone. Destroying the opposition of the church is necessary to conquering any Christian nation. Controlling the nation begins by bringing compromise in the altar and anesthetizing the church. Balaam was the first initiator of this approach and quickly gained his just reward. The doctrine of Balaam is being adopted by our once strong denominations as they accept homosexuality. Repent or face the judge of all the earth. The job of the remnant church is to pray the weight of the judicial throne on those claiming to lead God's people astray. Moses had to face leaders offering strange fire and God has not changed! Let the fire fall!

God set the boundaries for your life
Within this time and space,
Your habitation preordained
Marked for this very place.

A destiny He's called you to
To represent His Throne.
That's why the Father's more than pleased
To name you as His own!

PRAY AND OBEY

"Word At Work" Ministries makes available Bible studies without price. Those who receive them are asked to respond in relational obedience sowing simply as God directs. Books, CDs and DVDs are available for purchase through our online store at **wordatwork.org**.

"Pray and Obey" was birthed from the Father's heart for those in the church experiencing financial trauma, and all who may be suffering the temporary hardship of a limited or fixed income. We trust the covenantal obedience of those being blessed will cover others' lack. When nearly a third of the Body cannot afford teaching materials necessary for growth toward maturity, the remainder of us dare not ignore their cries. The same teaching in book, CD or DVD that can be purchased will also be available in Bible study format on (as schedule permits) a "Pray and Obey" basis.

"Pray and Obey" is an attempt to fulfill the Lord's direction in 2 Corinthians 8:12–15: *"For if there is first a willing mind, it is accepted according to what one has, and not according to what he does not have. For I do not mean that others should be eased and you burdened; But by an equality, that now at this time your abundance may supply their lack, and their abundance also may supply your lack—that there may be equality. As it is written, 'He who gathered much had nothing left over, and he who gathered little had no lack.'"*

"Pray and Obey" is a covenant of obedience—it is not a buy-sell agreement. It is important to realize God is serious about covenant. Just as God holds "Word at Work" Ministries accountable to offer the Word without price, the Lord will hold the receiver accountable to respond in obedience. May the Lord bless your study! *To access our library of teaching or place an order for study aids go to:*

wordatwork.org
"Word At Work" Ministries
P. O. Box 366, Placentia, CA 92871 USA
email: info@wordatwork.org

BIBLIOGRAPHY

Biblical definitions from *Theological Dictionary of the New Testament Vol. II.* Used by permission of Wm. B. Eerdmans Publishing Co.

Biblical definitions from the "Lexical Aids to Both the New and Old Testament" as published in the *Hebrew Greek Key Study Bible*. I highly recommend this edition for every believer. It can be purchased from AMG Publishers, Chattanooga, TN 37422.

Scriptures taken from the *Holy Bible, New International Version,* copyright 1973, 1978, 1984 International Bible Society. Used by permission of Zondervan Bible Publishers.

Definition taken from *American Dictionary of the English Language, Noah Webster 1828. Noah Webster's First Edition of an American Dictionary of the English Language.* Published by the Foundation for American Christian Education. Copyright 1967.

The Expositor's Greek Testament. Published by Wm. B. Eerdman's Publishing, 255 Jefferson SE, Grand Rapids, MI 49503, 1983.

The Amplified Bible. Zondervan Corporation, Grand Rapids, MI 49506. Copyright 1965.

Gesenius' Hebrew-Chaldee Lexicon to the Old Testament, translated by Samuel Prideaux Tregelles, LL.D., Baker Book House, Grand Rapids, MI. Copyright 1979.

Richard Francis Weymouth, *The New Testament In Modern Speech,* edited by Ernest Hampden-Cook, M.A., Third Edition, copyright 1911.

The Living Bible Paraphrased—Executive Heritage Edition, copyright 1979 by Tyndale House Publishers, Inc., Wheaton, IL 60187.

A Greek-English Lexicon of the New Testament, translated and edited by Walter Bauer, W.F. Arndt and F.W. Gingrich, published by The University of Chicago Press, Chicago, IL 60637.

Logos Bible Software, Scholar's Library, 1313 Commercial Street, Bellingham, WA 98225-4307.

The Theological Word Book of the New Testament, TWNT.

Al Houghton, *After God's Own Heart,* CD Series, Word At Work Ministries, P.O. Box 366, Placentia, CA 92871.

ABOUT THE AUTHOR

Al Houghton grew up in a small town in Missouri. He graduated from the University of Missouri at Columbia, with a Bachelor of Science Degree in Marketing. After graduation, he joined the Navy to become a pilot, flying 161 combat reconnaissance missions during the Vietnam War. He left the military to fly commercially, but God dramatically intervened, calling him into ministry.

In 1975, he moved to Southern California to attend seminary and earned a Master of Divinity Degree in theology. Immediately upon graduation, the Lord instructed him to start a teaching ministry and live by faith.

The teaching ministry began in home Bible studies, but grew to occupy other facilities, like Mott Auditorium on the campus of the U.S. Center for World Missions in Pasadena, where Al taught for ten years. Doors opened in other nations and Al began to minister at International Leadership Conferences from 1984 through 1987 which marked a transition as God added a prophetic touch to the teaching ministry.

A daily Bible study, entitled the "Word At Work," was begun in 1981 and today over two decades of daily Bible studies can be downloaded at **wordatwork.org**.

Al's current assignment is elevating the church into their kingly priesthood as "agents of justice." Many free nations stand at the crossroads of judgment or salvation, based on choices made. By invoking the covenant of "Sure Mercies," the church can impact those choices. Only a vibrant church who knows their covenant can confront political leaders in the power of the Spirit. Saving the nation means awakening the church to the power of their covenantal roots. The vision of "Word at Work" Ministries is to develop regional discipleship schools where future leaders can catch the fullness of covenant!

Al has authored five books: *Jesus and Justice*, *The Sure Mercies of David*, *Converts or Disciples?*, *Marked Men*, and *Purifying the Altar*.

JESUS & JUSTICE

Jesus paid the price for the church to function as *"Kings and Priests."* *Jesus & Justice* traces the development of the function of the priestly and kingly ministries. The primary passion of a priest was atonement or salvation, but kings had a very different assignment. Their God-given job was to judge and make war. Jesus in the gospels is the suffering servant priest who "turns the other cheek" to save. But when He ascended and took a seat at the right hand of God, He quickly became the Judge of all the earth.

Jesus & Justice restores to the church the authority of the resurrected King. The complete absence of any fear of God in our nation proves the church has lost its foundation for biblical justice. Christians represent the Jesus of Revelation and have an obligation to move God's hand against evil when it manifests in their presence!

The early church walked in this demonstration of justice from praying Peter out of jail to praying the political leader Herod into judgment. Paul accessed this judicial realm when a false prophet captured a Proconsul, but blindness on the false prophet persuaded the politician. **Jesus & Justice releases this level of authority in the church while outlining the preparational path necessary to stand in the fire you have to call down!**

All materials available from our secure online store at www.wordatwork.org
or by calling 714-996-1015

THE SURE MERCIES OF DAVID

How should believers respond to the avalanche of evil assaulting our nation, cursing our biblical culture and outlawing the voices of virtue?

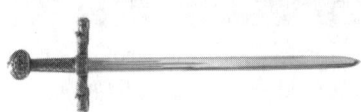

God covenanted with David to redeem his failure and cut off his enemies. David new what to ask for to save his land, based on this covenant. Jesus guaranteed the covenant of "Sure Mercy" and Paul preached it in Acts 13 with a warning that failure to use it could cost the loss of cities, and even the nation.

"Sure Mercy" empowers the church by putting a two-edged sword in the hand of every believer. The first edge cuts away the guilt, shame and insecurity of personal failure allowing God to transform the failure into a foundation for future prophetic fulfillment. The second edge moves God's hand to execute biblical justice saving the nation from all those intent on perverting and destroying the land by filling it with iniquity!

Learning the difference between "Sure Mercy" for an individual and "Sure Mercy" for a nation empowers us to pray an entirely different way. David expressed in the Psalms God's heart for victory and His willingness to war in our behalf. This book helps the church war spiritually as David did physically!

All materials available from our secure online store at www.wordatwork.org
or by calling 714-996-1015

MARKED MEN

God has promised end-time protections for His people as we navigate perilous times to accomplish a great end-time harvest. The prophetic tragedy of the last leadership generation is that they primarily equipped the church to recognize the mark of the counterfeit christ. The Bible promises nine real marks from the true Christ, eacah available for a specific end-time purpose. Almost every believer knows the counterfeit 666, but how many of us can name one of God's nine real marks enabling us to finish our call?

Some of the questions answered are:

1. If we gain God's marks, are we protected from premature death until we finish our heavenlyl assignments?
2. Will Jesus come to church before He comes for it, and if so, for what purpose?
3. If the cup has to be full before we can get a new heavens and earth, doesn't this make the pre-trib, mid- and post- arguments inconsequential?
4. Are we preparing our children for the wrong rapture? How should we be training them for the future?
5. How does the principle of fullness impact the church? Does fullness of iniquity demand fullness of Christ?
6. If in the end people must acquiesce to buy or sell, what must we do to achieve God's promised protection now?

All materials available from our secure online store at www.wordatwork.org
or by calling 714-996-1015

CONVERTS *or* DISCIPLES?

Converts or Disciples? is a prophetic word to the church, hopefully causing a reassessment of our ultimate purpose. If our number one goal is making disciples, then every believer we impact should be empowered to pass the 12-fold test of discipleship reflecting the commitment of the early church as they cultivated an apostolic culture!

The 12-fold Test of Discipleship

1. True discipleship begins when we choose to embrace _____.
2. Converts walk where _____ _____, while disciples walk where _____.
3. A convert sets his own _____, while a disciple embraces God's _____.
4. Converts often reject a _____ _____, while disciples accept it.
5. Converts use faith to _____ _____, while disciples use it to _____ _____.
6. Converts are oblivious to _____, while disciples discern it.
7. Disciples volunteer for _____, while converts hesitate.
8. Disciples dare not covenant with _____, but converts do it repeatedly.
9. Disciples are vigilant about who their actions _____, but converts are not.
10. Disciples escape financial manipulation because they give only by _____ need, while converts usually respond to _____ need.
11. Disciples display the _____ _____ _____ _____, while converts do not.
12. Disciples have to extend _____, while converts think it is optional.

All materials available from our secure online store at www.wordatwork.org or by calling 714-996-1015